The Justification of a Sinner

A Treatise on Justification by Faith Alone

wherein the truth of that point is fully cleared, and vindicated from the cavils of its adversaries

Delivered at Magdalen Hall in Oxford
by
William Pemble
Master of Arts

"And be found in Him, not having mine own righteousness, which is of the Law, but that which is through the faith of Christ, the righteousness which is of God by faith." Philippians 3:9

Edited by Dr. Don Kistler

Soli Deo Gloria Publications
. . . *for instruction in righteousness* . . .

Soli Deo Gloria Publications
A Division of Soli Deo Gloria Ministries, Inc.
P.O. Box 451, Morgan, PA 15064
(412) 221-1901/FAX 221-1902
www.SDGBooks.com

*

The Justification of a Sinner was first published in 1625 as *A Treatise on Justification*. This modern reprint was retypeset from the 1635 edition printed in London. This Soli Deo Gloria reprint, in which spelling, grammar, and formatting changes have been made, is © 2002 by Soli Deo Gloria. All rights reserved. Printed in the U.S.A.

*

ISBN 1–57358–129–1

Library of Congress Cataloging-in-Publication Data

Pemble, William, 1592?-1623.
 The justification of a sinner: a treatise on justification by faith alone : wherein the truth of that point is fully cleared, and vindicated from the cavils of its adversaries / by William Pemble.
  p. cm.
 Spelling, grammar, and formatting changes have been made to this reprint of the 1635 edition.
  ISBN 1-57358-129-1 (alk. paper)
  1. Justification (Christian theology) 2. Puritans   I. Title
BT764.3.P46 2002
234'.7–dc21

2002008085

Contents

Dedication   vii

To the Christian Reader   ix

Section I

Chapter 1   1
*The explication of the terms:
justice, righteousness, and sanctification*

Chapter 2   8
*In what sense the word "justification" ought to
be taken in the present controversy, and
the difference between us and our
adversaries therein*

Chapter 3   18
*Refuting our adversaries' cavil against
our use of the word "justification"*

Section II

Chapter 4   23
*The orthodox opinion concerning the manner of
justification by faith, and the refutation
of popish errors in this point*

Chapter 5   36
*Refuting the Arminian error, showing
that faith does not justify in a proper sense,
as it is an act of ours*

Chapter 6   45
*Refuting the popish doctrine that other
graces justify us and not faith alone*

Section III

Chapter 7   69
*The righteousness whereby a man is justified before God
is not his own or inherent in himself,
and in this life no man has perfection
of holiness inherent in him*

Chapter 8   87
*No man can perfectly fulfill the law in performing
all such works, both inward and outward, as
each commandment requires, against which
truth popish objections are answered*

Chapter 9   109
*No man in this life can perform any particular good work so
exactly that in every point it shall answer the rigor of the
law, provedby conscience, Scriptures, and reason.
Also, popish objections are answered*

Chapter 10   135
Three objections to the truth answered

Contents v

Section IV

Chapter 11   154
Justification by works makes void the covenant of grace; the difference between the law and the gospel, the use of the law, and the erroneous thinking of our adversaries in this point

Chapter 12   171
Bellarmine's erroneous distinction of the word "gospel"

Section V

Chapter 13   178
Justification by fulfilling the law overthrows Christian liberty

Chapter 14   184
Justification by works subjects us to the rigor and curse of the law

Section VI

Chapter 15   195
The reconciliation of that seeming opposition between St. Paul and St. James in this point of justification

Chapter 16   205
The confirmation of the orthodox reconciliation of St. James and St. Paul by a logical analysis of James 2

Section VII

Chapter 17   234
None can be justified by their own satisfaction for the transgression of the law; also, a brief summary of popish doctrine concerning human satisfaction for sin

Chapter 18   248
All sin is remitted unto us wholly in the fault and punishment for the satisfaction of Jesus Christ alone

Dedication

To the right worshipful Dr. Wilkinson (Principal of Magdalen Hall), the masters, bachelors, and other students of that flourishing society:

Sirs,

Custom has made dedicating books almost as common as printing them, and wisdom directs us to dedicate where we owe either respect or thanks. This work therefore is yours by right, the author whereof (who is now with God) undertaking it at your request and performing it among you for your good. Now to bestow it upon you is not a gift, but repayment. And I hope it will both stir you up to be careful to continue fitting men to stand up in his place, and remain to his successors as a pattern of imitation, if it is too high for emulation. To commend this author to you would be to bring owls to Athens, and for me to commend the work would not add much worth to it. I know nothing can disparage it except, perhaps, its naked margin without comment or commentary, but as you and all who will be pleased to take notice of his years and his great abilities in all human learning will confess, he could not have time to read many Fathers, and so that defect may be easily pardoned. For he had fully finished only six years of study, yet he had thoroughly traced the circle of the arts and attained to an eminence not only in those ordinary sciences, wherein all scholars have some smattering, but even in those sublimer speculations of which not all are capable and even fewer search after. For he was expert in mathematics, both applied and pure; his skill in history was also praiseworthy. He spent some time (and not without success) in learning foreign languages, and much time in the study of our home-taught tongues, so that he could have been a professor in either Greek or Hebrew, all which endowments, as they might afterwards have enabled him to read with much profit, so could they not help but prevent him in his younger years from reading all the ancient Fathers. So that it was not want, but abundance of learning that took up his time and prevented his writing in the margin, and therefore I hope shall not disparage this work. The first weapon young fencers learn to use is a single sword; when they are masters of that they enlarge their skill. Our author was but young; let it not prejudice him that he first used the sword of the Spirit, the Word of God, especially this that is so dexterously wielded, that by it alone he has fatally wounded the Romish Leviathan. Therefore (as is my knowledge) these lectures were heard with much applause; so do I persuade myself that they will be read with great approbation and will occasion the publishing of other lectures and private labors wherein he took no less pains, nor deserved less praise than in his public endeavors. So, hoping that you will accept these small pains of mine, I take my leave and rest.

Yours willing to do you greater, though not more acceptable service,

John Geree
Tewkesbury, July 9, 1629

To the Christian Reader

Gentle Reader,

This treatise was neither finished nor published by the author. He left it with me when he died to be dealt with as cause should require. Upon perusal, I found it fit for the time—so full of life, so sound and clear in proof, that in my thinking it will do much good. And here you have it as he left it. The argument is chiefly about the differences between us and Papists, and no controversy is more disputed and less agreed upon than this. Christ and His blood are the main cause of our spiritual peace. Papists and others divide with Him and take something to themselves. The spiritual pride that is in the heart of man would fain have a finger in the work of salvation. There are other controversies between us and the other party—some are for the Pope's kitchen, some for the Pope's crown—but this issue of our justification touches the life of grace to the quick and breeds more in our flesh than any. Those sicknesses are most dangerous that come from within. It is a fundamental issue wherein to fail takes away the essence of a Christian. There is now such need to have the world confirmed in this truth of God that I thought it good to send this book abroad wherein it is put out of question to any man of a clear eye that we are not justified by any thing we can do or suffer.

Many write books, and then confute them themselves when they are done. But as for our author, what he wrote he believed. Being about to die, he confirmed this truth in a discourse full of life and power, and professed to stake his life upon the belief that it was the very truth of God. We read that some learned Papists, when they are about to give up the ghost, disclaim their own merits and would find all in Christ alone. But our author did it before sundry persons, with that life and feeling and clear apprehension of the love of God in His Son that such as heard him, and loved him well and long, could not well tell whether they should weep or rejoice—weep to see a friend die or rejoice to see him die as he did.

Good reader, learn this holy instruction out of this book: we are not to be found in our own righteousness at all. Believe it and you shall have what he had, peace passing all understanding in life and in death. "Being justified by faith (not by works) we have peace with God," said Paul. If any ingenious, learned Papist would undertake to answer this book, I think I might prophesy thus: as Vergerius (Bishop of Capo d'Istria, and nuncio to Popes Clement VII and Paul III), reading Luther in order to refute him, was converted and had his soul saved, and as Pighius, though of a peevish enough spirit, yet, reading Calvin to confute Calvin, was in the very doctrine of justification confuted himself, and joined with us—so I say, would a modest Papist read this book to reply to it, he could not but see the truth and yield unto it. Though many have done excellently in this argument, yet to speak my opinion freely, at least for perspicuity, this surpasses them all. Farewell.

Yours in Christ,

Richard Capel

SECTION I

Chapter 1

The explication of the terms: justice, righteousness, and sanctification

Having by God's assistance in my prior treatise on the grace of faith dispatched two of the general points I had at first proposed, regarding the antecedents and the nature of true faith, we are now by the same help to go forward to the third general point, namely, concerning the consequences of faith, which are two: our justification with regard to God and our obedience with regard to ourselves. The former will show us how to judge the dignity and excellent worth of faith, being so far honored in God's gracious acceptance as to be made the blessed instrument of our spiritual peace and comfort, flowing from our justification. The latter will direct us how to make trial of the truth of our faith in the discovery of the inseparable union that exists between believing and obeying.

Let us begin with the former, our justification. I shall endeavor to deliver the doctrine to you as briefly and plainly as so large and difficult a subject will allow. Because explaining the word will give us some light for understanding the matter, we are first to see what is meant by the words "justification" and "justice" or "righteousness."

Justice, therefore, or righteousness (I mean that which is created, for of uncreated righteousness we have nothing to say) is nothing but a perfect conformity to and agreement with the Law of God. God's will, being originally, essentially, and infinitely righteous, must be the pattern and rule of all derivative and finite righteousness. Now this righteousness, though but one in its substance, nevertheless admits a twofold consideration, being called either:

1. Legal and of works, which stands in that conformity to God's Law which is inherent within ourselves, when in our own persons and works we possess and practice that righteousness which is required of the Law.

This legal justice is also of two types. First, it may be of obedience, when all such things are done as the Law commands and left undone which it forbids. He who does so is a just man. Or it is of punishment or satisfaction, when the breach of the Law is satisfied by enduring the utmost of such penalties as the rigor of the Law requires. For not only he who does what the Law commands, but even he also who suffers all such punishments as the Lawgiver in justice can inflict for the breach of the Law, is to be accounted a just man, and reckoned, after such satisfaction made is as no transgressor of the Law.

The reason for this is plain from the nature of penal laws. For, first, where the penalty is suffered, there the will of the Lawgiver is satisfied in that His will was that the Law should be observed or the punishment undergone. If therefore he to whom the Law is given does either, he satisfies the will of the Lawgiver. Had His will been absolute, so that nothing else could have contented Him

The Explication of the Terms

but obedience, then it would have been a vain thing to have prescribed a determinate penalty. But when a penalty is limited in case of disobedience, it is manifest that though the intent of the Lawgiver was obedience, yet it should suffice if there was satisfaction by bearing the penalty.

Second, the good and benefit of the Lawgiver are hereby also satisfied. For it is to be supposed in all penal laws that the penalty prescribed is every way proportionate and equivalent to that good which might accrue by the observation of the Law. Otherwise the wisdom of the Lawmaker could justly be questioned, as giving an apparent encouragement to offenders when they should see the penalty not to be as harmful to them as their disobedience was gainful. He therefore who suffers the penalty is afterward to be reckoned as if he had kept the Law, because by his suffering he has advanced the Lawgiver's honor or benefit as much as he could by his obeying.

2. Evangelical righteousness by faith, which is such a conformity to God's Law as is not inherent in our own persons, but, being in another, is imputed unto us and reckoned as ours. The righteousness of the Law and the righteousness of the gospel are not two different kinds of righteousness, but are the same in regard to the matter and substance thereof; they differ only in the subject and manner of application. The righteousness of works is that holiness and obedience which are inherent in our own persons and performed by ourselves. The righteousness of faith is the same holiness and obedience inherent in the person of Christ and performed by Him, but embraced by our faith and accepted by God as done in our stead and for our benefit.

These are the various meanings of the words "justice" or "righteousness" so far as they relate to the point in hand.

In the next place we are to inquire of this word "justification," which is nothing but making a person just or righteous. It may be taken in a double sense, for a person is made just by either infusion or apology. We will discuss it using these terms for want of better ones.

Justification by infusion is when the habitual quality of righteousness and holiness is wrought in any person by any means whatsoever, whether it is created and infused into him by the work of another or obtained by his own art and industry. Thus Adam was made just (Ecclesiastes 7:29), God having given him in creation the inherent qualities of justice and holiness. Thus also the regenerate are made just, inasmuch as by the Holy Ghost they are sanctified through the real infusion of grace into their souls, by which they increase also more and more by the use of exercise and all good means.

Justification by apology is when a person accused as an offender is judicially or otherwise acquitted and declared to be innocent of the fault, and so is freed from the punishment. When the innocence of a party accused is thus pleaded and declared, he is thereby said to be justified or made just according as, on the contrary, by accusation and condemnation a party is said to be made unjust. This is plain by Isaiah 5:23: "They justify the wicked for a reward, and take away the righteousness of the righteous from him." That is, they condemn the righteous, which is making them unrighteous in the sight and estimation of men. So 1 John 5:10: "He that believeth not God hath made Him a liar," because unbelievers in their heart call God's truth into question, and accuse Him of being false to His

Word. So again, Psalm 109:7: "When he is judged, let him be condemned"; literally, let him go out a wicked person, for so his condemnation makes him, that is, declares him to be. But here, further, it must be observed that this justification of a person by pleading before receiving absolution in judgment is of two sorts, according as the persons to be justified are likewise of two different conditions.

Some are truly and inherently just, being no transgressors of the Law, either not at all or not in that whereof they are accused. In this case, if any crime or suspicion of crime is laid to their charge, they are justified either by a plain denial of the fact, alleging that the fault whereof they are accused was never committed by them, or by denying the evil of the fact, alleging that in so doing they have done well because they have done what the Law commanded, and that is their warrant. Thus Samuel justified his government against all surmise of fraudulent and wrongful dealing that the people might imagine by him (1 Samuel 12:3). Thus David cleared himself before God from that crime of conspiracy against Saul his master, and seeking the kingdom (which Cush and other courtiers accused him of), professing his innocence and desiring God to judge him according to his righteousness and integrity in that regard (Psalm 7:3–4). We need no other examples of so plain a matter. Those who are justified by this means are justified by that righteousness which is of the Law and of works. By such a plea, though man may be justified before man, yet in the sight of God no flesh living shall be justified, as hereafter we shall see.

Some are not truly righteous in themselves, but are in their own person transgressors of the Law. These (when they are accused) have no other means whereby they may be justified but by confessing the crime and pleading satisfaction, that for their transgression against the Law and offense thereby against the Lawgiver they have fully satisfied by doing or suffering some such thing as by way of just penalty has been required of them. Now he who can plead such a full and perfect satisfaction ought therefore to be accounted innocent and free from all defect of further punishment (for it is supposed that he has endured the utmost evil the Law could inflict), and so he is to be esteemed as if he had not violated the Law at all. For plenary satisfaction for a fault and the non-commission of such a fault are of equal value, and deserve a like justification. In this point it must be noted that if the offended party pardons without any satisfaction being taken, the offender is not justified at all. And again, if the offense is such that there can be no satisfaction made, then it is utterly impossible that the offender should ever be justified.

Now this satisfaction which an offender may plead for his justification is threefold:

First, there is that which is made by himself in his own person. He who can plead this kind of satisfaction is justified legally by his own righteousness and merits.

Second, there is that which is made by another for him, when another, by consent and approbation of the party offended, interposes himself as surety for the delinquent party in his stead and name to make that satisfaction which is required of the party himself. Whether this is done by doing or suffering the same things which the delinquent should have done or suffered, or some other things of equivalent worth and dignity, he who pleads this kind of satisfaction is justified evangelically by grace through the righteousness of another imputed to him, and accepted as his.

The Explication of the Terms

Third, there is that which is made partly by himself and partly by another. This kind of satisfaction may have a place between man and man, but between God and man it has no place at all. Neither by this, nor by that first kind of satisfaction which is done in our own person, can any man be justified in the sight of God, but only by the second sort, that satisfaction which is made by another for us, as we shall see afterwards.

Chapter 2

In what sense the word "justification" ought to be taken in the present controversy, and the difference between us and our adversaries therein

Having thus distinguished the words, it follows that we inquire in which of the aforementioned senses we are to take this word "justification." The difference between us and our adversaries in the Roman Church is in this point very great and irreconcilable. They affirm that justification is to be taken in the first sense, that is, making a man just by the infusion of real holiness into him. So that, with them, to justify bears the same sense as to purify or sanctify, that is, to make an unclean, unholy, and unjust person formally or inherently pure, holy, and just, by working in him the inherent qualities of purity, sanctity, and righteousness.

On the contrary, we teach according to the Scriptures that justification is to be taken in the second sense for the pleading of a person's innocence that has been called into question, whereby he is judicially absolved and freed from fault and punishment. So that, with us, to justify a person is a judicial proceeding to acquit him of the crime whereof he is accused and to declare him free from the punishment he deserves. Which of us is in the right is very material to be determined, considering that all ensuing disputations concerning the justification of a sinner are to be framed upon one of these grounds rightly taken; an error here is like a misplaced thread at the beginning that runs awry afterward through the whole piece. Our adversaries plead for the assertion that the etymology of the word *justificare* is "to make just" in the sense (they say) as *purificare, mortificare, vivificare,* and many similar words signify "to make pure" or "to make dead or alive" (by the real induction of such and such qualities).

Again, they allege Scriptures. "They that turn many to righteousness (literally, justify many) shall shine as the stars forever" (Daniel 12:3). "He that is righteous (*justificatur*) let him be righteous still" (Revelation 22:11). "He saved us by the washing of regeneration, and renewing of the Holy Ghost . . . that being justified by His grace, we should be made heirs according to the hope of eternal life" (Titus 3:5–7). "And such were some of you; but you are washed, but you are sanctified, but you are justified in the name of the Lord Jesus, and by the Spirit of our God" (1 Corinthians 6:11). Out of these, with some other places such as Romans 8:30 and Hebrews 9 (but such as have scarce any show of good proof), they conclude that by justification nothing else is meant but the infusion of the habit of justice into him who was previously sinful and unjust.

Hereto we answer. First, as for the etymology, the meaning of words is to be ruled not by etymologies, but by the common use. Now it is a well-known thing that in the custom of all languages this word *justificare* imports nothing but the declaration of the innocence of a person and lawfulness of any fact, against such accusation as claims either an injustice or a wrong. "I will justify such a man or such a matter," say we in English, and no Englishman understands thereby anything but this: "I will make it appear that such a man is honest, such a fact is lawful, however questioned to the contrary."

In other languages, my skill serves me not, nor is it needful to trouble you with instances. Those who have written of this subject in every nation can witness for their own language. And further, this word *justificare* being of a latter stamp, unknown to such Latin authors as are of ancient and purer language, and fitted by ecclesiastical writers to express the meaning of those two words of the original Hebrew and Greek, it is apparent that the copy must follow the original, and the Latin word must bear the same sense as the Hebrew and Greek words do. And that this is the legal sense which we have spoken of is a point so manifest throughout the whole Bible that nothing but impudence can deny it, as we shall presently perceive.

For in the next place, as for the Scriptures which they allege for proof of their interpretation of the word, we answer that of a multitude of places of Scripture wherein the word "justify" is used our adversaries may truly pick out one or two or three that seem to favor their assertion of infusion of habitual justice, yet they gain little thereby. For where ten or more may be alleged against one in which the contrary meaning is used, reason tells us that an article and doctrine of religion ought to be framed out of the meaning of words and phrases which is usual, ordinary, and regular, and not out of that which sometimes comes in by way of particular exception. Might he not be judged destitute of sense and modesty who would quarrel at the significance of the word *ecclesia*, arguing that in the New Testament it is not used for the company and assembly of the faithful because in a place or two (such as Acts 19) it is taken for any ordinary civil meeting of people together? We grant them that Daniel 12 and Revelation 22 speak of being made just *formaliter*, by infusion of inherent holiness in a sinner. For so ministers may be said to justify many (as it is in Daniel), that is, by their ministry they may turn many to righteousness, directing them to the means of holiness and, as God's instruments, working in them the graces of conversion and regeneration. And so he who is just (as in Revelation) may be justified still, that is, may increase in the inward habit and outward exercise of holiness more and more. Thus we yield to them in these two places, without seeking other interpretations further off. And yet this will be no prejudice to our doctrine, which is grounded upon the other meaning so generally used.

We answer that, of all those other places alleged by Bellarmine and Becanus, there is not one that necessarily enforces such a meaning of the word as he and fellows stand for. These above the rest are most cited: 1 Corinthians 6, Titus 3, and Romans 8:30, where justification is, they say, combined as one and the same with sanctification and regeneration. I answer that they do ill to confound those things that the Apostle has distinguished very plainly. He tells the Corinthians that the unrighteous shall not inherit the kingdom of God, and that they had been such, even of the most notorious rank. But now they were washed, sanctified, and justified. By three words the Apostle expresses the change of their former condition. One is metaphorical: "you are washed"—the meaning whereof he declares in two proper words following: "you are sanctified," which represents one degree of washing or cleansing from the corruption of nature (in part) by the Spirit of our God, of whom is the gift of inherent grace, and, "you are justified," which is another sort of cleansing from the guilt of sin completely in the name of the Lord Jesus, that is, by the righteousness and merits of Jesus

Christ. Nothing can be more perspicuous and elegant.

Titus 3:5 is also as plain. God (says the apostle, speaking of the heirs and sons of God in Christ) has saved us, not by any works of ours, but by His own mercy. This salvation is set forth to us in the means and in the end. The means are two: regeneration and justification. He has saved us by the washing of regeneration and renewing of the Holy Ghost. This is the first means.

Regeneration is expressed by its properties or parts: washing, or doing away with the filthy qualities of our corrupted nature; renewing, or investing it with new qualities of graces and holiness.

Regeneration is also expressed by the efficient cause: the Holy Ghost, whom He has shed on us abundantly or richly, following the metaphor of comparing the Holy Ghost in this operation to water poured out.

Regeneration is expressed through the meritorious cause of it, through Jesus Christ our Savior, who has procured the sending down of the Holy Ghost into the hearts of the elect (verse 6). This is one step to heaven, our regeneration, but it is imperfect and cannot abide the severity of God's judgments. Now we must be absolutely free from all guilt before we can have hope of obtaining eternal life. Therefore follows the other means of salvation, our justification by the free grace of God, which utterly frees us from all blame whatsoever both of obedience to the law and of satisfaction for sins against the Law, that thus, being regenerate and justified, we might obtain the end of our salvation, eternal life.

The third passage is Romans 8:30: "Whom God has predestinated, those He has called; whom He called, He also justified; whom He justified, He also glorified." In this place Becanus declares triumph, for, he says, "The apostle

The Sense of the Word "Justification"

here describes the order of man's salvation, first in God's decree, then in the execution of it by three decrees of vocation, justification, and glorification. It follows necessarily from thence that either sanctification is left out or it is confounded with one of those three degrees named. It is a desperate shift to say that sanctification is signified by vocation or glorification; therefore it must be the same as justification, and this cannot be eluded."

We leave shifts to the Jesuits, returning him to this passage. The plain, direct answer is this: Sanctification is here comprised in the word "vocation," for the links of this golden chain are inseparable, and all those who are called must be justified and glorified. By vocation must here be meant that calling which is inward and effectual, not that alone which is outward by the external ministry of the Word. For all who are thus called are not justified, as is apparent. And, again, some, such as infants, are justified who are not capable of such a calling. But now, wherein stands the inward vocation of a sinner? Is it not in the infusion of the inherent, sanctifying grace, enlightening his eyes, opening his ear, changing his heart, and turning him from darkness to light, from the power of Satan to the obedience of God? In a word, is it not the renovation of his faculties? What else is it but sanctification, or regeneration, or conversion? It is called "vocation" only with regard to the means whereby it is ordinarily effected, that is, the preaching of the Word. He must coin some new mystery in divinity who will persuade us that some other work of grace is meant by vocation and not that of sanctification. Therefore we have neither one link snapped out, nor two shuffled together in this chain of our salvation, but four as distinct as they are indivisible: election; sanctification (whereto we are called by the gospel preached, as in

2 Thessalonians 2:14), justification by faith, which is a fruit of sanctification and glorification.

The fourth passage is Hebrews 9:13–14: "For if the blood of bulls and goats, and the ashes of a heifer sprinkle them unclean, sanctifieth as touching the purifying of the flesh, how much more shall the blood of Christ, who through the eternal Spirit offered Himself without fault to God, purge our consciences from dead works, to serve the living God?"

Hence, they argue that as the Levitical sacrifices and washing sanctified the flesh from outward legal impurity, so the sacrifice of Christ purges the conscience from inward spiritual uncleanness of dead works or sins. This purging of the conscience is nothing but the justification of a sinner.

To this I answer that the apostle, in that chapter and the next, explaining the virtue and efficacy of Christ's death, and that it far exceeds the force of all Levitical sacrifices (the shadows of it), ascribed unto it what could not be effected by those, that is, eternal redemption (verse 12), purging of the conscience from dead works (verse 12), the putting away of sin (verse 26), the sanctification of the elect (10:7, 10), and making them heirs according to the hope of eternal life. In neither of these passages then is our sanctification combined with our justification, but both are distinctly declared as two different parts of grace and means of the accomplishment of our eternal happiness. It is scarcely worth the labor to examine those other Scriptures produced by our adversaries, whereof some parts directly contradict, and the rest only seem to confirm their assertion.

In general, therefore, this much we confidently affirm: let the concordance be studied, and all those places examined wherein either *sadeq* is used in the Old or *dikaion* in the New Testament, and there will not be found one instance, no, not one, in which those words carry any other meaning than that which we assert, that justification is the clearing of a party's innocence which has been questioned as faulty and blameworthy. Consider a few examples:

Justification is sometimes applied to God, when man justifies God (Psalm 51:4; Romans 3:4). Wisdom is justified by her children (Matthew 11:19). And the publicans justified God, being baptized with the baptism of John (Luke 7:29). Can there be any other meaning of justification here but this one, that God is then justified when His works, His wisdom, and His sacred ordinances, being accused by profane men of being untrue, unequal, unjust, and foolish, are acknowledged by the godly, or any other means evidently declared unto all men, to be full of all truth, equity, wisdom, and holiness?

Justification is sometimes applied to man:
- Before man in things between man and man. "If there be a controversy between men, and they come unto judgment, that the judges may judge them, then they shall justify the righteous, and condemn the wicked" (Deuteronomy 25:1). "Woe to them which justify the wicked for a reward, and take away the righteousness of the righteous from him" (Isaiah 5:23). "He that justifies the wicked, and he that condemns the just, even they both are an abomination to the Lord" (Proverbs 17:15). "Oh, that I were made judge in the land, that every man that has any suit or cause might come to me, and I would do him justice" (2 Samuel 15:4). In these and many like places, to justify is a judicial proceeding to absolve a party from fault and blame, whether it is rightfully or wrongfully done.

"Be confounded and bear your shame, in that thou

hast justified your sisters," speaks God to Jerusalem, in comparison to whose abomination the sins of Sodom and Samaria were scarcely to be accounted any faults (Ezekiel 16:52). They were saints compared to her. Of the Pharisees Christ speaks, "Ye are they that justify yourselves before men, but God knows your hearts" (Luke 16:15). That is, "You give an appearance of outward holiness, and deem it sufficient to make it appear before men that you are holy, without regard to acquitting the sincerity of your hearts before God."

• Before God, where God justifies man: "The innocent and the righteous slay not, for I will not justify the wicked" (Ezekiel 23:7)—by esteeming him as innocent, and letting him go from punishment. "He is near that justifies me; who will contend with me?" (Isaiah 50:8), said the prophet in the person of Christ, signifying that God would make it appear that He was blameless for the rejection of His people the Jews, who perished for their own sins and not His fault. "As by the offense of one judgment came on all men to condemnation, so by the righteousness of one the free gift came upon all men unto justification of life" (Romans 5:18). "Who shall lay anything to the charge of God's elect? It is God that justifies; who shall condemn?" (Romans 8:33–34). "I know nothing by myself, yet in this am I not justified; He that judges me is God" (1 Corinthians 4:4). Paul says here, "I have kept a good conscience in my ministry, but God is my judge. Though my conscience pronounces me innocent, yet God is the only one who judges me and my conscience." There is also Acts 13:38–39: "Through this man is preached unto you the forgiveness of sins, and from all things from which you could not be justified by the Law of Moses; by him all that believe are justified."

By these places (not to name more) it appears plainly that justification is opposed to accusation and condemnation, and therefore can signify nothing else but the defense and absolution of a person accused of being an offender. This is so clear and evident that it cannot be gainsaid except by those alone who are willfully blind and obstinately resolved to contradict any truth that stands against their inveterate errors.

We may not, we dare not shut our eyes against such clear light; nor ought we to be so bold, when God has acquainted us with His meaning, as to follow another of our own making. And therefore, according to the Scriptures, we acknowledge and maintain that as in other places where mention is made of the justification of a sinner before God, so in Romans 2 and 4, and in Galatians 3 (where the doctrine thereof is directly handled), by justification nothing else is meant but the gracious act of Almighty God whereby He absolves a believing sinner who has been accused at the tribunal of His justice, pronounces him just, and acquits him of all punishment, for Christ's sake.

Chapter 3

Refuting our adversaries' cavil against our use of the word "justification"

Our adversaries have little to reply against such plain passages. Something they *do* answer is:

It cannot be denied but that justification many times bears that sense we stand for. But withal, they would have us observe this rule: God cannot declare a man to be just, but of an unjust man he must make a just man. And they give this reason: because "the judgment of God is according to truth" (Romans 2:2). We embrace this rule and the reason for it, acknowledging that wherever there is justification there must be justice in some way or other in the party justified. But the question still remains in what manner God makes a sinner just whom He in judgment pronounces so to be. They say that it is by bestowing on him the grace of sanctification and perfect righteousness inherent in his own person. We affirm that it is by imputing unto him the perfect righteousness of Christ, accepting Christ's obedience for his own. Amidst our differences, let us come as near them as truth will give leave. Thus far we go along with them.

There is inherent righteousness bestowed upon a sinner whereby from an unholy, impure, and unjust man he is made holy, clean, and just. We all confess this work of the Holy Ghost, renewing man in the spirit of his mind, restoring in him the image of God in knowledge, righteousness, and holiness (Ephesians 4:24; Colossians 3:9). The Holy Ghost dwells in the elect as in temples dedicated to His service, which He adorns by communicating unto them His heavenly graces (1 Corinthians 3:16 and 6:19; 2 Corinthians 6:16; Romans 8). He makes them living members of Christ's body and fruitful branches of that true vine (Romans 12:5; 1 Corinthians 12:11; John 15:4). This grace infused is a fountain of living water springing up to eternal life (John 4:14). These things we believe and teach.

The Popish doctors call "foul" on our Reformed writers, charging Calvin and others with denying all inherent righteousness in believers and maintaining only an imputed righteousness outside them. We tell them it is a gross calumny forged by perverse minds, who do not wish to understand men's plainest writings. Neither Calvin, nor anyone who ever maintained the truth with him ever denied the righteousness of sanctification. Calvin holds this, and we also hold, with the Scriptures, that the righteousness which justifies us in God's judgment is not in ourselves but is all in Christ.

Inherent righteousness or sanctification always keeps company with justification in the same person. They are never severed in their common subject, a true believer, as appears in Romans 8:30. But that therefore they must be combined as one and the same grace and work of God may be affirmed with as good reason as that sunlight and heat are all one because they are always joined together.

By this grace of inherent righteousness, a man is in some sense justified before God; that is, so far as a man by the grace of God has become truly holy and good, so far God esteems him holy and good. God takes notice of His own graces in His children. He approves and gives testimony of them in case it is needful, as appears by the righteousness of Job, David, Zechariah, and other holy men who *were* good and *did* good in God's sight. Yea, in the life to come, when (all corruptions being utterly done away) the saints shall be invested with perfection of inherent holiness, by the righteousness of their own and not by any other, they shall then appear just in God's sight.

Thus far we agree with them. But herein we differ: although by infusing the grace of sanctification God makes him righteous and holy in some measure who was before altogether unholy and wicked, nevertheless we affirm that, by and for this holiness, the best of living saints never was nor shall be justified in God's sight, that is, pronounced just and innocent before the tribunal of His justice. For we here take up the aforenamed rule laid down by our adversaries: Whomever God pronounces to be perfectly just must be made perfectly just, for God's judgment is according to truth. Now that no man in this life is made perfectly just by any such inherent holiness in him as is able to withstand the severe and exact trial of God's judgment is a truth witnessed to by the Scripture, and confessed always by the most holy saints of God. Our adversaries indeed stiffly plead the contrary, teaching that sin and corruption in the justified are utterly abolished. The error and pride of this imagination we shall shortly have occasion at greater length to reveal unto you. Meanwhile, let this much suffice: man, being not made perfectly just in himself, cannot thereby be declared perfectly just before God; and therefore some other righteousness, and not that of sanctification, is to be sought for, whereby a sinner may be justified in God's sight.

To that argument of ours from the opposition of justification to accusation and condemnation, confirmed by so many passages of Scripture, they answer that this hinders nothing at all. Both, they say, may be agreeable to God, who in His mercy justifies some, that is, makes them inherently just, and of His justice condemns others, that is, punishes them.

To these slight answers we make this short reply: where words are opposite (as they acknowledge these to be), according to the laws of opposition, they must carry opposite meanings. But unto accusation, condemnation, and punishment, nothing is opposite but defense, absolution, and pardon. Where therefore *justificare* is coupled with these words, it must bear this and no other meaning. To make a good man out of a bad man is not the opposite of accusation, condemnation, or punishment of him. He may be accused, condemned, and punished justly, and later made good.

I will not trouble you with more of their cavils. Let this much suffice for the clearing of this point, that justification and sanctification are to be distinguished and not confounded. The righteousness of the one is in us, in its nature true and good, but as for its degree and measure imperfect, and always yoked with the remainder of natural corruption. And therefore, if a sinner should plead this before the judgment seat of God, offering himself to be judged according to this righteousness and innocence, oh, how soon his mouth would be stopped, and this confession wrung from out of his conscience: "All my righteousness is as filthy rags!" And again: "I am vile; what shall I answer Thee!" That other righteousness of justification is outside us in Christ's possession, but it is ours by God's gracious gift and acceptance; and this is in every way perfect and unreproved in the severest judgment of God. Therefore, when a sinner is drawn before the bar of God's judgment, accused by the Law, Satan, and his conscience, convicted by the evidence of the fact, and now to be sentenced and delivered to punishment by the impartial justice of God, in this case he has to allege for himself the all-sufficient righteousness of a mighty Redeemer, who alone has done and suffered for him that which he could never do nor suffer for himself.

This plea alone, and no other in the world, can stop up the mouth of hell, confute the accusations of Satan, chase away the terrors that haunt a guilty conscience, and appease the infinite indignation of an angry Judge. This alone will procure favor and absolution in the presence of that Judge of the whole world. This alone brings down from heaven into our consciences that blessed peace which passes all understanding. We rest secure from fear of condemnation, being provided a defense that will not fail us when after death we come into judgment.

SECTION II

Chapter 4

The orthodox opinion concerning the manner of justification by faith, and the refutation of popish errors in this point

Having thus cleared the meaning of the word "justification," and having shown that when the Scriptures speak of the justification of a sinner before God we are to thereby understand the absolution of him in judgment from sin and punishment, we are now upon this ground: to proceed, in the further explication of this point, to inquire by what means and in what manner this justification of a sinner is accomplished. That we may go on more distinctly, I will organize all our ensuing discourse of this point under three headings.

First, I will touch on the condition required in those who shall be justified.

Second, I will touch on the matter of our justification, what righteousness it is whereby a sinner is justified.

Third, I will touch on the form of justification, in what the quality of this judicial act of God in justifying a sinner consists.

1. The condition required in such as shall be partakers of this grace of justification is true faith, whereunto God has ordinarily annexed this great privilege that by faith and only by faith a sinner shall be justified. To this the Scriptures witness in terms as direct and express as any can be. "We conclude that a man is justified by faith without the works of the law" (Romans 3:28). "For we say that faith was imputed unto Abraham for righteousness" (Romans 4:9). "Being justified by faith, we have peace with God through Jesus Christ our Lord" (Romans 5:1). And there are other similar passages. Whence it is agreed upon all sides *that* a sinner is justified by faith, but regarding the manner *how* he is said to be justified by faith there is much controversy and brawl between the orthodox of the Reformed churches and their adversaries of Rome and Holland, the Papists and the Arminians.

The sentence of the Reformed churches concerning this point consists of two branches:

First, a sinner is justified by faith, not properly as it is a quality or action which by its own dignity and merit deserves at God's hands remission of sins, or is by God's favorable acceptance taken for the whole and perfect righteousness of the law which is otherwise required of a sinner, but only in relation to the object of it, the righteousness of Christ, which it embraces and rests upon.

Second, a sinner is justified by faith in opposition to the righteousness of works in fulfilling the law, whereby now no man can be justified.

In this relative and inclusive sense the Reformed churches take this proposition: a man is justified by faith. They explain themselves thus: there are two covenants that God has made with man, by one of which and by no other means in the world salvation is to be obtained. The

Orthodox Opinion Concerning Justification by Faith

one is the covenant of works, the tenor whereof is "do this and you shall live." This covenant is now utterly void in regard to us who, through the weakness of our sinful flesh, cannot possibly fulfill the condition of obedience required thereby; and therefore we cannot expect justification and life by this means. The other is the covenant of grace, the tenor whereof is "believe on the Lord Jesus and you shall be saved." The condition of this covenant is faith; the performance of it differs from the performance of the condition of the other covenant.

"Do this and live" is a compact of pure justice, wherein wages are given according to debt so that he who does the work of obeying the law may in strict justice, for the work's sake, claim the wages, eternal life, as being justly deserved. "Believe this and live" is a compact of freest and purest mercy, wherein the reward of eternal life is given to us in exchange for that which bears not the least proportion of worth with it. So that he who performs the condition cannot yet demand the wages as due unto him in severity of justice, but only by the grace of a free promise, the fulfilling of which he may humbly sue for. By the grand difference between these two covenants clearly expressed in Scripture it appears manifestly that these two propositions, "a man is justified by works" and "a man is justified by faith," carry meanings utterly opposite to one another. The one is proper and formal, the other metonymical and relative.

In this proposition, "a man is justified by works," we understand everything in proper and precise terms. A righteous man who has kept the law exactly in all points is, by and for the dignity and worth of his obedience, justified in God's sight from all blame and punishment whatsoever, because perfect obedience to the moral law in itself, for its own sake, deserves the approbation of God's severe justice and the reward of heaven.

But in that other proposition, "a man is justified by faith," we must understand all things relatively. A sinner is justified in the sight of God from all sin and punishment by faith, that is, by the obedience of Jesus Christ believed in and embraced by a true faith. This act of the justification of a sinner, although it is properly the work of God alone for the merit of Christ alone, yet is it rightly ascribed unto faith and faith alone, forasmuch as faith is the main condition of that new covenant which we must perform if we will be justified. So by the performance thereof we are said to obtain justification and life, for when God by grace has enabled us to perform the condition of believing, then do we begin to enjoy the benefit of the covenant; then is the sentence of absolution pronounced in our consciences which shall be later confirmed in our death and published in the last judgment.

Second, our faith and no other grace directly respects the promises of the gospel, accepting what God offers, sealing the truth thereof by assenting thereto, and embracing the benefit and fruit of it unto itself by relying wholly upon it. This interpretation of that proposition the Reformed churches admit and no other, rejecting as erroneous and contrary to the Scriptures such glosses as ascribe anything to the dignity of faith or make any combination between faith and works in the point of our justification. Among these there are three erroneous assertions regarding man's justification by faith, which we will briefly examine and refute.

(1) Faith justifies us as a proper, efficient, and meritorious cause, which by its own worth and dignity deserves to obtain justification, remission of sins, and the grace of

well-doing.

This is the doctrine of the church of Rome, which Bellarmine labors to prove in the seventeenth chapter of his *First Book on Justification*, where, disputing against justification by faith alone, he tells us: "If we could be persuaded that faith justifies, then we would never deny that love, fear, hope, and other virtues justify us as well as faith." Whereupon he sets out to prove that there is in faith itself some efficacy and merit to obtain and deserve justification. His arguments are chiefly two.

His first argument is from those places in Scripture wherein a man is said to be justified: through faith (Galatians 2:16); in faith (Romans 5:1); by faith (Romans 2:8; 4:2; 3:20; James 2); or absolutely without article or preposition (which would mean through faith, out of faith, or by faith). These prepositions signify, he says, the true cause of our justification, which he proves, first, by the contrary, when a man is said to be justified by works. This notes the true, efficient, deserving cause of his justification. He proves his point further by other passages where we are said to be redeemed, saved, and sanctified, through Christ, through blood, through death, through wounds. In Hebrews 11 the saints are said to do such and such things by faith, all signifying the proper cause.

His second argument is from those passages of Scripture which, he says, plainly show that faith effects remission, and indeed merits it due to its own intrinsic meriting worth. Such are these: "your faith has saved you" or "your faith has made you whole." Christ used these words often, such as to the woman who washed His feet in Luke 7:50, to her who had an issue of blood in Matthew 9:22, to the blind man who recovered his sight in Mark 10:52, and to the Canaanite woman: "O woman, great is thy faith" (Matthew 15:28).

Now see what the merit of this faith was. "For this saying, Go thy way; the devil is gone out of thy daughter" (Mark 7:29). "Thus Abraham, being strengthened in faith glorified God," who therefore justified him for the merit of his faith (Romans 4:20). And again in Hebrews 11, by many examples we are taught that by faith, that is by the merit and price of faith, Enoch and other men pleased God (Hebrews 11:5–6).

For answer hereunto:

Unto the argument from the proposition we reply that if "by faith and works" must be strictly taken in the same kind of causality, then the Jesuits would do well to stick to that and make the similitude between faith and works run thus: as a man is justified by works, that is, for the proper and only merits of his obedience, so a man is justified by faith, that is, for the only merit of his believing in Christ; and by that means both shall be true and effectual causes of justification. But if Bellarmine dares not thus press the similitude for fear of being found guilty of despising the blood of the New Covenant, attributing that to the merit of faith which belongs only to the merit of Christ, he must then give us that leave to distinguish what he takes to himself. And if he falls to his qualifications and modes, he must pardon us if we also seek such an interpretation of those places as may not contradict other Scriptures, which testify that we are justified by His grace through the redemption that is in Christ (Romans 3:25), that all sin is purged by the blood of Christ, that by the sacrifice of Himself He has put away sin, and that with His offering He has consecrated forever those who are sanctified (Hebrews 1:3). We dare not without horrible sacrilege ascribe the grace of our justification unto the work and worth of anything whatsoever in ourselves, but wholly to the righteousness of Christ.

And therefore when the Scriptures say we are justified by faith, we do not take the word "by" in the formal and legal sense that we are justified by the efficacy of our faith, or for the worth of our faith, according as it is understood in justification by works. Rather, we take it relatively and instrumentally, that we are justified by faith, that is, by the righteousness of Christ, the benefit whereof unto our justification we are made partakers of by faith as the only grace which accepts the promise and gives us assurance of the performance. He who looked to the brazen serpent and was cured might truly be said to be healed by his looking, though this action was no proper cause working the cure by any efficacy or dignity of itself, but was only a necessary condition required of those who would be healed upon the obedient observance whereof God would show them favor.

So he who looks on Christ, believing in Him, may truly be said to be saved and justified by faith, not for the worth and by the efficacy of that act of his, but as it is the condition of the promise of grace that must necessarily go before the delivery of it to us, upon our obedience whereunto God is pleased of His free grace to justify us. Nor is this figure of speech in any way harsh or unusual to grasp: the opposite on behalf of the opposite, the thing related on behalf of the correlate, the appearance or sign on behalf of the object itself. In sacramental locutions it is a general custom to use the sign to represent the thing signified, and the like is used in other passages: "And the word of God grew" (Acts 6:5–7); "the mystery of faith" (1 Timothy 3:9); "in the words of faith" (1 Timothy 4:6); and "hope that is seen is not hope" (Romans 8:24).

And if we do not wish to be contentious, it is plain enough that in those places where the apostle treats justification by faith, that is, the grace of God in Christ, opposing works and faith, that the law and the gospel, the righteousness of the law to the righteousness of the gospel, this is nothing other than the righteousness of Christ. Thus faith is taken in Galatians 3:23 where he expressly treats justification: "Before faith came, we were kept under the law, shut up unto the faith which should afterward be revealed." That is, before Christ came, and the clear exhibition of the gospel and the righteousness thereof, the Church was kept under the ceremonial law as under a schoolmaster, which directed her unto Christ so that we might be justified by faith, that is, not by the lesson of the law but by Christ, typified and figured unto us therein.

Unto the other argument proving the merit of faith, we reply that there is in those places no ground at all for such a conceit. "Your faith has saved you," said Christ to some whom He cured in both body and soul. But what? Was it by the efficacy of faith and for the worth of their faith that this was done? No, as it was virtue going out of Christ that cured their bodily diseases, and His compassion that moved Him to it, so it was His grace and merits and free love that healed their souls and brought them pardon of their sins in the sight of God. Yet He says that their faith saved them because *by* believing the Son of God they received this favor, though it was not *for* their believing that they deserved it.

God bestows mercy where He finds faith, not because faith merits such favor at His hands, but because He is pleased to disperse His favors in such an order as He has appointed and upon such conditions as He thinks good. With regard to the Canaanite woman, her great faith could not claim by merit that favor which Christ showed unto her daughter, but Christ was pleased to honor her faith by His testimony of it and to help the daughter at the mother's entreaty. Christ did it upon that request of hers, so insistent and full of faith. But yet who can say she merited anything at Christ's hands by her faithful and persistent petition? If she were yet living she would deny it; and she does deny it there, counting herself a dog who is unworthy of the children's bread, when yet she believed strongly, and was a child of Abraham according to the faith.

To their statement that Abraham gave glory to God (and Enoch and others pleased God) by faith, we answer that it is one thing for a man to glorify and please God by his obedience; it is another to think that by so doing we deserve anything at His hands. If God in much grace and favor accepts the honor and contentment we are able to give Him by our faith and obedience, it does not follow that therefore we must in justice merit something at His hands.

Other arguments are offered as well, but they are so weakly knit that they fall asunder of themselves. Against them we have to cite the Scriptures that so often say we are justified freely by grace. And the Council of Trent, which they respect more than the Scriptures, has stated this: "We are therefore said to be justified gratuitously, because none of those things that precede justification, whether faith or works, merit the grace of justification" (Session 6, chapter 8). How then can they say faith merits justification?

Here our adversaries have two shifts to run to whereby they would avoid the absurdity of this assertion.

This merit, they say, is not from us but from God, because faith is the gift of God's grace. Therefore, though we are justified by merit, yet we are justified by grace because merit is of grace. It is because of grace that our faith has merit.

This, you may be sure, is some of that smoke from the bottomless pit wherein hell vented out the Jesuits, and their dark imagination, all to confound whatever is clear in Scripture. Scripture opposes these pairs: grace and nature, grace and merit (Romans 11:6). The Pelagians of old confounded nature and grace, teaching that we were saved by grace, yet affirmed that we are also saved by nature and the natural strength of free will. They solved the problem in this way: to be saved by nature is to be saved by grace, for nature is of God's grace and giving. In the same way, the papists confound grace and merit, making a thing meritorious because it is of grace. Faith merits because it is God's gracious gift. Nothing is more contradictory. If it is His gift, how does it merit, or from whom? From man it may, but from God it cannot, unless we will senselessly affirm that the gift deserves something from the giver. Is he who gives a hundred pounds freely thereby bound to give a hundred more? Had they said that faith is good because of God's giving, that would be true, and we may grant them that God is honored and pleased with His own gifts. But that every good thing merits, and that we can deserve something from God by His own gifts, is affirmed without all reason or Scripture, and will never be proved by either.

But there is another shift. Our adversaries also argue that faith merits justification, not because of its worthiness, but because of its fitness; that is, God in justice is not bound to bestow justification where there is faith, but yet in fitness He ought to do it. So that if He does not justify him who believes, He is likely to omit something very fit and agreeable. This distinction is a mere imposture and collusion.

Bellarmine, in dealing with it, seems to have a dog by the ear. He is loath to lose him, yet knows not how to hold him. If he is asked where Scripture makes the least intimation of such a distinction, he refers you to divines— that is, Popish schoolmen—who out of their own imagination have forged it and in time made it authentic. But he sticks in the mire when he tries to show what merit of condignity and merit of congruity are. Merit of condignity is works to which wages are due from justice. What, then, are merits of congruity? Such works whereto wages are not due by any justice. For example, he who labors the whole day in a vineyard merits a penny of condignity because in justice his labor is worth his hire. But he who for an hour's work receives a penny deserves it of congruity, because, though his labor is not worth it, yet he was promised a penny by him who sent him to work. Nothing can be more ridiculous and contrary to common sense than this, for the merit of any work is the proportion of its worth with the reward. Now in reason, wherein arises this proportion of any work with that reward? Does it stand in the dignity of the work itself or in the compact made between him who works and him who rewards? It is apparent that the work is deserving or not deserving according to its own nature, not according to a compact made. He who promises one person more for a little work than another for a great deal of the same kind does not, by such a compact, make the little labor of the one more deserving than the other's great pains. We must look to the work, what it is in its own nature, and, as it is of some worth or no worth, so account it deserving or not deserving.

When in the distinction they make some merits to be of condignity or worthiness, and others of congruity, or of fitness without worthiness, they offend in two ways grossly against two rules of reason. First, they oppose terms that are not opposite, worthiness and fitness being the same, if you take them with regard to the work. That which deserves a reward worthily deserves it fitly (how else is it worthy of the reward if the reward is not fit for it?), and that which deserves it fitly (if it deserves) deserves it worthily.

Moreover, they make their distinctions using terms that do not serve these distinctions, making worthiness apply to merit only while fitness belongs to compact. In plainer English, the distinction runs thus: merits are of two sorts. Some are merits indeed and deserve because they are worthy of a reward; others are not merits and do not deserve, because they are not worthy of the reward, but obtain it only with regard to compact and promise. For this rule is most certain: a work which deserves nothing by its own worthiness can never deserve anything by compact or promise. The Jesuits are senseless in defending the contrary.

If, said Bellarmine, a king promised a beggar £1,000 a year upon no condition, then indeed the beggar does not deserve it. But if upon condition he should do some small matter, as that he shall come to the court and fetch it, or bring a posey of flowers with him, now the beggar deserves it and may come to the king and tell him that he has merited his £1,000 a year. Every man but a Jesuit would say that it would be extreme impudence in a beggar to make such a demand so derogatory to the king's gracious bounty. Nor can it help them to say that a promise binds unto performance, so that God should be unjust and untrue if He did not bestow the reward promised, although

Orthodox Opinion Concerning Justification by Fa...

the works are not equal to the reward. For God's justice and truth in performing His promise do not imply our merit in performing the condition.

We do not deserve by our well-doing simply because God is just in His rewarding. And the reason is manifest: God in making the promise respected merely the freeness and bounty of His own grace, not the worthiness of our works. And therefore that obligation whereby He has tied Himself to performance is founded merely in His own truth, not a jot in our merit. When they tell us that faith merits justification by half a merit, they entrap themselves in a gross contradiction, since to deserve by half a merit is not to deserve it at all, but only to receive the reward by mere promise, God having promised to justify believers.

So much for the first assertion, that faith is the proper cause of justification, working it by its own efficacy and merits.

Chapter 5

Refuting the Arminian error, showing that faith does not justify in a proper sense, as it is an act of ours

2. The second error about this point is from the Arminians, with whom the Papists also agree. It is that we are justified by faith in a proper sense, that is, the act of believing, in that the credit is imputed to us for righteousness, being accepted of God and accounted unto us for that whole righteousness of the law which we were bound to perform. So that, according to this view, our very faith is that righteousness for which we are justified in the sight of God.

The authors of this opinion are Faustus Socinius, that unhappy heretic, in his most blasphemous book, *Concerning Christ the Savior,* and Michael Servetus, a Spaniard, in his second book, *Concerning Law and Gospel,* which errors are refuted by Calvin in *Little Works.* A stiff defender of this opinion was Christophorus Osterodius, a Polonian, in his disputations, *Against George of Tradel,* who for this and other pestilent errors about the article of man's redemption was, with his companion Andreas Vaidonitus, banished to the Low Countries where he has seated himself and published his opinions. Arminius and his followers have been chief promoters of it.

Arminius himself, as in other opinions of his, so in the publishing of this one, used much closeness and cunning conveyance. In his private disputations, published under the title *Concerning Justification*, he seems plainly to condemn it, saying that it is an abuse to say that faith is the formal cause of justification, and an error to affirm that Christ has earned for us that we are justified by the worthiness and merit of faith. In his public disputation he opens himself somewhat plainly, yet darkly enough (Thesis 19 on Justification; Thesis 7; Thesis 48.3.2). These are his words: "Justification is indeed attributed to faith, not because that would be justice, and because then the faith itself could be set against the rigid and severe judgment of God—although it is pleasing to God—but because in judgment mercy, triumphing over judgment, would obtain absolution from sins and be graciously imputed as righteousness. By the cause of this thing, first, God is just and merciful, then Christ (by His obedience, sacrificial offering, and intercession) is following after God in His good favor and command."

Here faith itself is imputed for righteousness. But it is not in God's severe judgment, but in His judgment of mercy. Faith in itself is not worthy, but yet Christ, by His merits, has deserved so that God will graciously accept it. This opinion, once published, was quickly contradicted, whereupon Arminius made known his mind in plainer terms. In his *Declaration of My Opinion to the Rulers of Holland and West Frisia,* he confessed that in the forenamed "Thesis," his meaning was that "faith itself, preeminent alongside of the mandate of the gospel, is imputed in the presence of God in, or for, righteousness, and that in grace, since this would not itself be the righteousness of the Law." And in his *Response to the 31 Articles,* he branches out his opinion into three distinct propositions (Article 4):

1. Christ's righteousness is imputed to us.
2. Christ's righteousness is imputed as righteousness.
3. To believe is imputed as righteousness.

The first of these propositions he grants, that Christ's righteousness is imputed to us. The second he denies, that Christ's righteousness is imputed for righteousness. The third he grants, that the act of believing is imputed for righteousness. Here are mysteries in the propositions hereafter to be unfolded.

We now meddle with the last, which is yet once more roundly expressed by Arminius in his epistle *To Hippolytus, the Principal Legate of the Pope:* "To believe is itself an act of faith, I say, to be imputed as righteousness, and that in its own proper sense, not metonymically." The same is the opinion of his fellows, the Remonstrants, of Vorstius (*Antibel. pap.* 106), of Peter Bertius (*Corrections with Sib. Lubber*), of Episcopius (*Thesis on Justification*), and the rest, with whom Bellarmine agrees fully (*Book 1 on Justification,* chapter 17). Commenting upon Romans 4, which says that Abraham's faith is imputed as righteousness, he says, "Where faith itself is judged to be righteousness, through this (i.e., through this judgment) faith does not lay hold of Christ's righteousness, but faith in Christ itself is righteousness." In sum, their opinion runs thus: God, in the legal covenant, required exact obedience to His commandment; but now, in the covenant of grace, He requires faith, which in His gracious estimation stands instead of that obedience to the moral law which we ought to perform. This comes to pass by the merit of Christ, for whose sake God accounts our imperfect faith to be perfect obedience.

This assertion we reject as erroneous, and in place thereof we defend this proposition: God does not justify a man by faith properly, imputing unto him faith in Christ for his perfect obedience to the law, and therefore accounting him as just and innocent in His sight, which we prove by these reasons:

1. We are not justified by any work of our own. But believing is an act of our own; therefore, by the act of believing we are not justified. This reason is most manifest by the Scriptures, which teach that we are saved by grace (Ephesians 2:5). And therefore it is not by the works of righteousness which we had wrought (Titus 3:6), "for if it be of works, then were grace no more grace" (Romans 11:6).

The corollary is likewise evident, that faith is a work of ours. For though John 6:29 says, "This is the work of God, that you believe in Him whom He has sent," yet our adversaries conclude thence that faith is God's work within us, and not our work by His help. For so would they run into that absurdity which they fasten upon us, that is, that when a man believes it is not man who believes, but God who believes in him. To believe, though it is done by God's aid, yet requires us to do it, and the act is properly ours; and, being so, we conclude that by it we are not justified in God's sight.

Here two objections may be made.

First, one may say that we are not justified by any work of our own, that which we ourselves do by our own strength without the help of grace. But we may be justified by some work which we do by the aid of grace, and such a work is faith.

We answer that this distinction of works done without grace is a trick to elude the force of such Scriptures as exclude indefinitely all works from our justification, without distinguishing either the time when they are done or the aid and help whereby they are done, whether by nature or by grace. It is without all ground in Scripture to thus interpret these propositions. A man is not justified by works, that is, by works done by the power of nature before and without grace. A man is justified by grace, that is, by works done by aid of grace. These interpretations are mere forged inventions of froward minds, affirmed but not proven, as we shall more fully declare later.

Second, they may say that though we are not justified by any works of our own, that is, by any works of the law, nevertheless by a work of the gospel, such as faith is, we may be justified. "You would prefer that I be disquieted where there is need of so many remedies," says Erasmus in another case. It is a certain sign of an untrue opinion when it must be bolstered up with so many distinctions. Nor yet has this distinction any ground in Scripture or in reason; for both tell us that the works commanded in the law and the works commanded in the gospel are one and the same for the substance of them. What work can be named that is enjoined us in the New Testament which is not also commanded us in that summary precept of the moral law: "Thou shalt love the Lord thy God with all thy heart, and with all thy soul, and with all thy strength, and with all thy mind, and thy neighbor as thyself" (Luke 10:27; Deuteronomy 6:5)? What sin is there against the gospel that is not a transgression of the law? If the gospel commands charity, is it any other than that which the law commands? If the gospel commands faith, does not the law enjoin the same?

You will say, "No, it does not command faith in Christ."

I answer that it does. For that which commands us in general to believe whatever God shall propose unto us, commands us also to believe in Christ, as soon as God makes it known it is His will that we should believe in Him. The gospel reveals unto us the object; the law commands us the obedience of believing it. Wherefore faith, as the substance of the grace and works done by us, is a work of the law, and so to be justified by the action of believing is to be justified by works and by our own righteousness, contrary to Philippians 3:9: "That I may be found not having mine own righteousness . . . ."

2. God counts that only for the perfect righteousness of the law which is so in deed and truth. But faith is not the perfect fulfilling of the law; therefore God does not account it as such. Our adversaries grant the latter clause, that faith is not the exact justice of the law, such as can stand before the severity of God's judgments. The former must be proved, that God does not account that for perfect justice which is not perfect indeed. This appears from Romans 2:2: "The judgment of God is according to truth." Where therefore anything is not truly good and perfect, there God does not esteem it so.

Here also it will be objected that God sometimes judges according to exact justice, and then He judges nothing to be perfectly just but that which has true perfection of justice in it. But sometimes He judges according to mercy, and so He may esteem a man perfectly righteous for that which is not perfect righteousness in itself, namely for his faith.

Surely this is a trim distinction which, when applied, sets God's mercy and truth together by the ears. Who would say that when God judges out of mercy He then does not judge according to truth? The Scriptures do not acquaint us with any such merciful judgment of God. This they do acquaint us with: God judges according to mercy, not when He pronounces and declares a sinner to be perfectly righteous for that righteousness which is truly imperfect, but when He judges a sinner to be righteous for that righteousness which is perfect, but is not his own. In this judgment there is both truth and mercy: truth in that He esteems me to be perfectly righteous for that righteousness' sake which is every way perfect, and mercy in that He accepts for sin that righteousness which is performed for me by Christ my Surety—but it is not my own. As for other merciful judgments of God besides this we acknowledge none.

3. We are not justified by two righteousnesses existing in two various subjects. If we are justified by the work of faith, we shall be justified partly by that righteousness which is in us of faith, and partly by the righteousness of Christ without us. Therefore we are not justified by faith properly.

"The righteousness of faith is inherent in us, and by it we are justified," say our adversaries. In contrast, say the Scriptures, the righteousness of Christ is inherent in Him, and by it we are justified. "Being now justified by His blood, we shall be saved from wrath through Him" (Romans 5:8). "By the obedience of one, many shall be made just" (Romans 5:19). Wherefore either we are properly justified by both faith and the righteousness of Christ, or there is an error, and one part must stand out. We cannot be properly justified by both, by our own faith and by Christ's obedience too. For if we are perfectly just in God's sight because of our own faith, what need is there for the imputation of Christ's obedience to make us just? On the other hand, if by Christ's righteousness we are perfectly justified, how can God account us to be perfectly just for our faith?

Arminius and his friends, seeing that these things cannot stand together, have (according to the good will which they bear toward the righteousness of Christ) kept our faith in and thrust Christ's obedience out, denying utterly that it is imputed unto us for righteousness. But, my brethren (who, I hope, make a better choice), let us part with our own righteousness, leaning wholly upon the righteousness of Christ, seeking the comfort of our justification in His perfect obedience, and not in our weak and imperfect faith.

These reasons may suffice to show the terror of the assertion that we are justified by faith by its own proper sense, God accepting the act of believing for the perfect obedience of the law. And therefore, in those places where it is said that faith is imputed for righteousness, the phrase is to be expounded metonymically; that is, Christ's righteousness, believed on by faith, is imputed to the believer for righteousness.

Our adversaries say that faith, of its own dignity and merit, does not obtain this favor of God, so as to be esteemed as the perfect righteousness of the moral law. But this comes to pass only by the merits of Christ, who has procured this grace unto us so that God should thus accept our faith.

We answer that this is affirmed, but it is not proven. They speak a little more favorably than the Romanists, who make faith itself to actually merit justification. These other adversaries would have faith not merit justification, but graciously accepted for righteousness. But we do not find in Scripture any such doctrine as that Christ has earned merit that we should be justified for our faith, or Christ has merited for our faith, so that faith should be esteemed by God for fulfilling that perfect justice of the law whereby we are justified in God's sight.

These things the Scriptures do not teach! They teach that Christ is our righteousness, and that we are justified by His blood and obedience. But that He has merited by His obedience that we should be justified by our own obedience and righteousness is a perverse assertion of men who love to run about the bush, and, leaving the straight way, run in crooked and froward ways. It differs little from the like shifts of the disciples of Rome, who, to maintain the merit of our works and of Christ too, solve it with this trick: Christ has merited that we might merit. But as we acknowledge no other merit but that of Christ, so we acknowledge no other righteousness leading to justification but this one.

Chapter 6

Refuting the popish doctrine that other graces justify us and not faith alone

3. The third and last issue of controversy between us and those of Rome is their assertion that a sinner is not justified by faith alone, but also by other virtues and graces such as hope, love, repentance, and the fear of God.

This we also reject as an error contrary to the Scriptures, whereby we are taught that a man is justified by faith alone. To discover the truth of this point, you must call to mind the different meanings of the word "justify," as it is taken by us and by our adversaries.

With them, "to justify" is all one with "to sanctify"—from unjust and unholy, to make one inherently just and holy. With us "to justify" is "to absolve an offender, acquitting him of blame and punishment." According to these different meanings, this proposition (that a man is justified by faith alone) has a double meaning. One is that a man, by faith alone, is inherently sanctified; another meaning is that a man, by faith alone, obtains absolution in God's judgment from all fault and punishment. Only this latter meaning is true, and it is that only which is defended by us of the Reformed churches, namely that faith alone is the grace of God whereby a sinner, believing the promise, and resting himself upon the righteousness of Christ, receives mercy from God in absolving him from the fault and punishment of all his transgressions, and is accounted righteous for Christ's sake. This gracious privilege God has annexed unto faith, as unto the condition of the New Covenant, and not unto love, hope, fear, repentance, or any other grace. For not these, but faith only respects the promise of the gospel.

The former sense of that proposition is false and absurd, namely that a man by faith alone is inherently sanctified. Nor do any of the Reformed churches maintain such a construction thereof. Wherefore, when Bellarmine and his accomplices dispute eagerly against justification by faith alone, those arguments wherewith they suppose to smite through the truth of our assertion are let fly at a wrong mark. They are all aimed at this target, that is, to prove that a man is sanctified by other inherent graces as well as faith. This point we easily yield to them, confessing that inherent righteousness consists not of one grace, but the manifold graces of God's Spirit wrought in the heart of such as are regenerate (1 Peter 4:10).

Nevertheless, to clear up some points which may be doubted, let us briefly take a view of the chief passages of Bellarmine's long discourse, which he maintains from the twelfth chapter of his first book, *De Justificatione*, to the end, to prove that a man is not justified by faith alone. Of his arguments, which are few, I shall name only three which are material.

ARGUMENT 1. If other virtues justify as well as faith, then it is not by faith alone; but other virtues *do* justify. The latter assertion he proves out of the Council of Trent (Session 6, chapter 6), where seven preparatory graces to justification are reckoned:

1. Faith.
2. The fear of God.

3. Hope in His mercy.

4. The love of God as the fountain of justice (and in the manner of a benefactor, says Bellarmine).

5. Repentance, a sorrow and detestation of sin.

6. A desire to receive the sacrament of baptism.

7. A purpose to lead a new life and keep God's commandments.

All these, says Bellarmine, justify a man, preparatorially, antecedently, regularly ordered. Faith is the root and beginning of our justification; the rest follow in order. All must go before as needful preparations, and justification follows as the effect of all of them together, not by faith alone. The Jesuit goes over every particular to show by Scriptures what force each of those graces has in justification. But it is not worthwhile to repeat his proofs. Unto this argument we answer two things:

1. It is framed upon the error which puts out of frame the whole dispute of our adversaries about this article of justification, namely that regeneration and sanctification are all one thing with justification, and that to justify a sinner is nothing but to do away with inherent corruption by infusion of inherent righteousness. This we have heretofore by the Scriptures cleared to be false; and therefore this argument proving our sanctification to be wrought by other graces as well as by faith touches not the point of justification in the remission of sins, which faith alone obtains through the promise.

2. Regarding these graces which they make preparatory unto justification, that is, to sanctification, we answer that it is a philosophical dream of such as measure out the works of God's Spirit in man's conversion according to Aristotle's *Physics*. It is related to those disputes over previous or foregoing dispositions that qualify the matter for

receiving of the form. We acknowledge that in man's regeneration all graces of the Spirit are not perfected at once. But like the joints and sinews in the body, so the graces of sanctification in the spiritual new birth are at first weak and feeble, and over time they gather more strength according to our growth in Christ. But yet these are true as to the substance, though imperfect in their degrees and measure. There is now true spiritual life in such a one who was previously dead in sin, although there is not the free and able exercise of all the vital powers. Health there is, but not entirely free from all degrees of sickness or every kind of disease. Wherefore we affirm that these virtues, which are reckoned by our adversaries only as dispositions unto regeneration, are, if they are true and not counterfeit, the main parts and fruits of regeneration.

Hence we believe that these are foul errors which teach that a man without grace, by the power of his free will, may dispose himself to his regeneration by believing in Christ, fearing and loving God, hoping in His mercy, repenting of his sins, resolving upon amendment, and all this with true and sincere affection. It is equally false to teach that, if a man cannot do these things of his own mere strength and free will, yet he may, by the special aid of God inciting and helping him, do them while he is utterly unsanctified and in a state of sin; that true faith, fear, hope, love, repentance, and purpose of reformation are virtues and graces in a man who is yet graceless and without virtue because he is destitute of sanctification; or that these graces, consisting in the inward motion of the soul and change of the affections, are wrought in man not by any sanctifying grace of the Holy Ghost inwardly touching the heart, but by some other kind of virtue and aid (they do not know what)—external, exciting and helping forward the strength of nature.

All these are monstrous and misshapen imaginations, bred in proud hearts that would fain share the glory of their conversion between God's grace and their own free will; and they are maintained by curious heads whom philosophical speculations have transported beyond the simplicity of divine truth. Scripture speaks otherwise of these graces, as belonging to such as are not on the way to being made good, but are made so already.

"You are all the children of God by faith in Jesus Christ," says the Apostle Paul (Galatians 3:28). "Whosoever shall confess that Jesus is the Son of God, God dwells in him and he in God" (1 John 4:15); and "Whosoever believes that Jesus is the Christ is born of God" (1 John 5:1). Do we by true faith become the children of God, born of Him, in whom He dwells and we in Him, when in the meantime we are yet unsanctified, unholy, unclean, and not in the state of grace?

Bellarmine will prove that a man may have faith yet not be the child of God, out of John 1:12: "As many as received Him, to them He gave power to become the sons of God, even to them that believe on His name." See, he says, they who believe are not yet, but have power if they wish to become the sons of God, that is, by going on further from faith to hope and love, and the rest of the Tridentine dispositions. For it is love properly, and not faith, that makes us the sons of God; or so he would prove (contrary to that express passage in Galatians) out of 1 John, where the apostle has much excellent material, but nothing to *that* purpose.

With regard to that place in John, we answer that the Jesuit plays with the ambiguity of the word *exousia*, which is not here a liberty to do what we wish, as if we could at our pleasure become God's adopted sons, but is a right and privilege which Christ the natural Son bestows on true believers to be made God's adopted sons, and so co-heirs with Him of the heavenly inheritance. When is this privilege of adoption bestowed? When they believe, and as soon as they believe, before they are regenerate? No, John denies it. He gives power to be the sons of God, even to those who believe in Him. Who are they? He answers in verse 13: "which were born not of blood, nor of the will of the flesh, nor of the will of man, but of God." Faith then is not a preparative to justification, but a part of it.

And is not fear of God too? No, says Bellarmine, it is the beginning of wisdom, that is, of perfect justification (Psalm 111:10; Proverbs 1:7). This is a bad interpretation, but a worse argument. It is the beginning, and therefore not a part, he argues. Nay, if the fear of God is the alpha of Christian graces, certainly it thus constitutes one letter of that alphabet. It is such a beginning of wisdom as itself is wisdom too; otherwise God Himself deceives us who said, "Behold, the fear of the Lord, that is wisdom, and to depart from evil is understanding" (Job 28:28). And therefore, to take it in the Jesuit gloss, the fear of God is justification as well as the beginning of it.

For hope, it if is true, is that which makes not afraid (Romans 5:5); it is the anchor of the soul, sure and steadfast; it enters within the veil (Hebrews 6:18). It would be known what difference the Jesuit will put between that hope which is in a man before and that which is in him after his sanctification. If he says it differs only in degree, then he grants that it is the same in substance; whence we have a fair position that man, sanctified and unsanctified, is alike capable of the saving graces of God's Spirit.

The like we say for love of God (if it is sincere and

bred in the heart without dissimulation), upon those spiritual considerations not only of God's mercy in Christ, but also of His justice and infinite righteousness. For as the Trent fathers would have this love respect God as the fount of righteousness, we affirm this spiritual love is not to be found but in those hearts that are in some measure regenerate and made spiritual, in whom this love of God is shed abroad by the Holy Ghost that is given to them (Romans 5:5), as the apostle says.

This Bellarmine is soon forced to grant, yet he puts it off with a distinction. No man can love God perfectly with all his heart without the Holy Ghost, he concedes; but he may love God imperfectly without the Holy Ghost dwelling in him, though not without the special aid of God. Whereto we answer that it is one thing to love God perfectly and another to love Him truly. To love Him perfectly is to love Him with all the heart, all the soul, all the mind, and all the strength, which we grant that no man can do without the Holy Ghost. But we also affirm that no man did or shall ever do it in this life so long as there is lustful corruption in him causing the least aversion of his soul to God in any motion thereof. So that if none have the Holy Ghost abiding in them but such in whom love is thus perfected, He must be confined with the saints in heaven and not have His dwelling with the faithful on earth. But if imperfect love of God is also from the Holy Ghost dwelling in the hearts of the godly, who love God truly in unfeigned uprightness of heart, though in much imperfection by reason of sin, which diverts the heart unto other pleasures, then it must be known of the Jesuit what he means by imperfect love. Is it false love, such as mere natural man may conceive upon general grounds, that God is good, the chief good, just, holy, and full of all excellence? He will not say, for shame, that this is a true preparative unto justification. Is it true love, but in its degree imperfect, not so vigorous, so vehement, so hot as coals of Juniper, yet such as has some strength and warmth of spiritual affection? Then we require these men to draw us out a line by the rule of the Scriptures, and to tell us how far the true love of God may come without the grace of the Holy Ghost sanctifying the heart, whereas after it is past such a degree there is required the sanctifying grace of the Holy Ghost for it.

It will trouble their mathematics to describe unto us in what degree of perfection that woman's love was situated whose example they allege for a proof of this point out of Luke 7:47: "Her sins, which were many, are forgiven her, for she loved much." Can Bellarmine tell us how much this was, so that, by this pattern we may know how far men go in the true love of God before they are at all sanctified by inherent grace? For such wonders they would make us believe concerning this penitent sinner, that when her soul was full of faith and love for Christ, her heart full of sorrow, and her eyes full of tears for her sins, yet for all that she was a graceless, unholy person, whose love, faith, and sorrow came not from the sanctifying grace of the Holy Ghost, but from free will, helped with some kind of external aid of God.

We have not faith to believe such mysteries as these. Nor yet in the last place can we conceive how there should be true repentance, with a sincere purpose of reformation and obedience, where the heart is not changed and renewed by the Holy Ghost. That godly sorrow and hatred of sin should spring out of a graceless heart, or that so holy a resolution of amendment of life should be in an unholy person, are assertions so contradictory and jarring

Refuting Justification by other Graces

that no Christian ear can with patience endure to hear them.

We conclude, then, regarding these dispositions unto sanctification, that if these graces are true, they are parts and chief branches of inherent righteousness. But if they are false and counterfeit, they are not so much as preparations thereunto. So much for this first argument, wherein yet one of these seven dispositions first reckoned up is omitted, namely, a desire to receive the sacrament of baptism. That is, a man who is baptized in his youth must later, before he is justified, have a desire to be rebaptized. For what is it for one baptized to desire to receive that sacrament again? This idea is so absurd that while Bellarmine reckons it up among the other dispositions, because of the authority of the Council of Trent, yet Becanus plainly abandons it, numbering these forenamed six graces only, choosing rather to venture the Council's credit than his own by defending an unreasonable position.

ARGUMENT 2. If faith alone justifies us, then it may do it when other graces are absent as well as when they are present. For since the virtue of justifying us depends upon faith alone, and since in this act it receives no aid from any other grace, it follows that it does not need the company of any other grace, as in the law of sense. If the whole force of burning proceeds only from heat, then where heat is, though there are no other qualities, yet there will be burning. Yea, if faith alone has force to justify, it will follow that it may justify not only in the absence of other graces, but in the presence of the contrary vices. For as the absence of other graces does not hinder, so the presence of other vices will not hinder faith one jot in its office of justifying. But it would be absurd to affirm that faith can justify without other virtues and with other vices; therefore the force of justifying is not in faith alone.

We answer that this sophism is fashioned upon the same block as the former, namely, that to justify and sanctify are all one. In this sense we confess the consequence is unavoidable. If faith alone, by its own virtue and force, sanctified, then it would effect this not only in the absence of other graces, but in the presence of their contrary corruptions; and the similitude which we bring to illustrate our assertion would confirm that of the adversaries. It is the eye alone that sees, say our men, yet the ear is in the head too.

Yes, they reply, but the eye could see well notwithstanding the ear being deaf. It is the heat alone of the fire or sun that warms, though there is light joined with it.

True, they say, but if there were no light, yet if heat remained it would warm just like the heat of an oven or of hell burning, though it shines not. You hold in your hand many seeds (it is the old comparison of Luther using Genesis 15); I inquire not what it is together, but what is the virtue of each one singly.

Yes, reply our adversaries, that is a needless question indeed. For if among those many seeds there is one with such sovereign virtue that it alone can cure all diseases, then it is no matter whether you have many or few or none at all of any other sort in your hand. You have that which, by its own virtue without other ingredients, will work the cure; nor do you have any answer in this case, for if as the eye sees, heat warms, and seeds and other items cure by their own proper virtue, so faith alone by its own efficacy did sanctify us.

But there is the error: faith works not in our sanctification or justification by any such inward power and virtue of its own, from whence these effects should properly follow. For in sanctification, faith, as we have seen, is part of that inherent righteousness which the Holy Ghost has wrought in the regenerate; and it is opposed to the corruption of our nature which stands in infidelity. Faith sanctifies not as a cause, but as a part of infused grace, and such a part as goes not alone, but is accompanied by all other graces such as love, fear, zeal, hope, and repentance, inasmuch as man's regeneration is not the infusion of one, but of the habit of all graces. Again, it is not the virtue of faith that justifies us; the grace of justification is from God, and He works it, but it is our faith that applies it and makes it ours. The act of justification is God's work, but our faith alone brings us its benefit and assurance.

Justification is an external privilege which God bestows on believers, having therein respect only to their faith, while grace alone has peculiar respect to the righteousness of Christ and the promise in Him. Whereby it is manifest that this argument is vain. Faith alone is respected in our justification; therefore faith is or may be alone without other graces of justification. Bellarmine would undertake to prove that true faith may be severed from charity and other virtues. But we have heretofore spoken of that point, and have shown that true faith without a form is dead and without a soul, and is a contradiction as vain as a true man without reason or a true fire without heat. We confess indeed that the faith held by the Jesuits (the same as that of Simon Magus) may very well be without charity and all other sanctifying graces, just a bare assent to the truth of divine revelations because of God's authority. As it is in devils, so it is in papists and other heretics. But we deny that this deserves the name of true faith, such that whosoever has it also has eternal life, as in John 6:47.

ARGUMENT 3. That which Scripture does not affirm is false doctrine. But the Scripture does not affirm that we are justified by faith alone. Ergo, to teach it is to teach false doctrine.

This argument touches the heart of the matter, and if this argument could be proved we must yield; for the Jesuits think their point is clear. Where is there any one place in all the Bible that says faith alone justifies? They even laugh at the simplicity of the heretics (as they christen us) who glory finding the word "only" in Luke 8:50 in that speech of Christ to the ruler of the synagogue: "Fear not, believe only, and she shall be made whole."

And much sport they make themselves with Luther, claiming that to help his case, by plain fraud he foisted into the text of Romans 3 the word "only." When caught with that fact, and when required to give a reason, he made answer according to his modesty, "I want thus, I order thus, the intention of my will stands in the place of reason." It is true that Luther in his translation of the Bible into the German tongue read the 28th verse of the chapter thus: "We conclude that men are justified without the works of the law, only through faith." This word "only" is not in the original. In so doing, if Luther did not fulfill the office of a faithful translator, yet he did the part of a faithful paraphrasing, keeping the sense exactly in that alteration of words. And if he is not free from blame, yet, of all men, the Jesuits are most unfit to reprove him, whose corrupting of all sorts of writers, divine and human, has long been notorious and infamous throughout Christendom.

What Luther's modesty was in answering those who found fault with his translation, we cannot say. The impudent forgeries of this generation witness abundantly that it is no rare thing for a lie to drop out of a Jesuit or a friar's pen. But be that as it may, it is not Luther's translation, nor that passage in Luke 8, that our doctrine of justification by faith alone is founded upon. We have better proofs than these, as shall appear unto you in the confirmation of the second cause of this syllogism: Whatsoever the Scriptures affirm is true doctrine; the Scriptures affirm that a man is justified by faith alone; therefore thus to teach is according to the word of wholesome doctrine.

Our adversaries demand proof of the clause. We allege all those places where the Scriptures witness that we are justified by faith without the works of the law.

These passages include: "Therefore we conclude that a man is justified by faith without the works of the law" (Romans 3:28).

"If Abraham were justified by works, he has whereof to glory, but not before God. For what saith the Scripture? Abraham believed God, and it was counted to him for righteousness" (Romans 4:2-3).

"For if they which are of the law be heirs, faith is made void, and the promise made of none effect, because the law works wrath; for where no law is, there is no transgression" (Romans 4:14-15).

"Knowing that a man is not justified by the works of the law, but by the faith of Jesus Christ, even we have believed in Christ, that we might be justified by the faith of Christ and not by the works of the law, for by the works of the law shall no flesh be justified" (Galatians 2:16).

"Is the law then against the promises of God? God forbid. For if there had been a law given which could have given life, verily righteousness should have been by the law. But the Scripture has concluded all under sin, that the promise by the faith of Jesus Christ might be given to them that believe" (Galatians 3:21–22).

For by grace you are saved through faith, and that not of yourselves; it is the gift of God; not of works, lest any man should boast" (Ephesians 2:8–9).

"Yea, doubtless, and I count all things but loss for the excellency of the knowledge of Christ Jesus my Lord, for whom I have suffered the loss of all things, and do count them but dung, that I may win Christ, and be found in Him, not having my own righteousness, which is of the law, but that which is through the faith of Christ" (Philippians 3:8–9).

Titus 3:5–7 also speaks of the righteousness which is of God by faith.

From these places, not to name more, expressly touching this point of our justification, we argue thus: A man is justified either by the works of the law or by faith in Christ. But he is not justified by the works of the law. Ergo, he is justified only by faith in Christ.

In this disjunctive syllogism, they cannot find fault with us for adding the word "only" in the conclusion, which was not in the premises. For reason will teach them that the two terms are immediately opposite; if one is taken away, the other remains alone. So in every disjunctive syllogism whose major proposition stands upon two terms immediately opposite, if one term is removed in the proposition, the conclusion is plainly equivalent to an exclusive proposition.

For example, we argue thus: either the wicked are saved or the godly. But the wicked are not saved. Thence it follows in exclusive terms that the godly only are saved. Similarly, in this case, our adversaries cannot deny that the proposition (a man is justified either by works or by faith) consists of terms immediately opposite. For otherwise they accuse the Apostle Paul of a lack of logic who should conclude falsely that "a man is justified by faith without works" (Romans 3:28) if he is justified either by both together, or else by neither. Seeing that he opposes faith and works as being incompatible, and excludes works from justification, we conclude infallibly by the Scriptures that a man is justified by faith alone. This argument is not avoidable by any sound answer, and puts our adversaries to the shifts. Yet rather than yield unto the truth, they fall unto their distinctions, whereby, if it were possible, they would shift off the force of this argument. Therefore the Scriptures oppose works and faith, the law of works and the law of faith, our own righteousness which is of the law, and the righteousness of God by faith. This manifestly tells us that we are justified not by works, by the law of works, nor by our own righteousness of God by faith. Our adversaries have a distinction to solve this matter with. They say, then, that works are of two sorts:

1. Some go before grace and faith, and are performed only by the strength of free will, out of that knowledge of the law, whereunto men may attain by the light of nature, or the bare revelation of the Scriptures. These works or this obedience to the law, which a mere natural man can perform, is (they say) that righteousness which the Scriptures call our own. By this kind of righteousness and works, they grant, none is justified.

2. Some follow grace and faith, which are done by man's free will, excited and aided by the special help of grace. Such obedience and righteousness is, they say, called the righteousness of God because it is wrought in us of His gift and grace. And it is by this righteousness that a man is justified.

By this invention they turn aside with a wet finger all

those Scriptures that we have alleged. We are justified, they agree, not by the works of the law, that is, by the obedience of the moral law which a man may perform without God's grace. But we are justified by the faith of Christ, that is, by that obedience of the moral law which a man may perform by faith and the help of God's grace. Boasting is excluded, says the apostle, by what law? By the law of works (that is, by the law performed by the strength of nature)? Nay, for he who performs the law by his own strength has cause to boast of it. By what law then? By the law of faith, that is, by faith which obtains God's grace to fulfill the moral law. Now he who obeys the law by God's help has no cause to boast (Romans 3:27). Israel which followed the law of righteousness could not attain unto the law of righteousness (Romans 9:31–32). Wherefore? Because they sought it not by faith; that is, they sought not to perform the law by God's grace, but as by the works of the law, that is, by their own strength. Thus Paul desires to be found in Christ, not having his own righteousness which is of the law, that is, that righteousness he performed without God's grace before his conversion, but the righteousness of God which is by faith, i.e., that righteousness which he performed in obeying the law by God's grace after his conversion.

To confirm this distinction, and the interpretations thereon grounded, Bellarmine brings three reasons to show that when works and faith are opposed, all works of the law are not excluded.

First, it is manifest that faith is a work, and that there is a law of faith as well as works. If therefore (Romans 3) all works and all law are excluded from justification, then to be justified by faith would be to be justified without faith.

Second, it is plain that the apostle (again in Romans 3)

intends to prove that neither the Jews by the naked observance of the law of Moses, nor the Gentiles for their good works before they were converted to the faith of Christ, could obtain righteousness from God.

Third, the apostle shows (Romans 4:4) what works he excludes from justification, namely, such whereto wages is due by debt, not by grace. Now works performed without God's help deserve reward out of debt, but works performed by His help deserve wages out of gratitude.

I doubt not but (notwithstanding these seeming reasons) the forenamed distinction and expositions of Scripture according thereto appear unto you at first sight to be strange, uncouth, and far from the intent of the Holy Ghost in all those aforementioned passages of Scripture. Let us examine it a little more narrowly, and you shall quickly perceive that in the schoolmen's distinction there is nothing but fraud and shifting (by works done by the strength of nature we are not justified; by works done with the help of grace we are justified). This is the distinction. Resolve it now into these terms which are more proper and it runs thus: a man is not sanctified by those works of the moral law which he does without grace, but a man is sanctified by those works of the moral law which he does by grace. Both sentences are squint-eyed, and look quite awry from the apostle's aim in this dispute regarding justification. Is it his intent in Romans 3 to prove that a sinner destitute of grace cannot be made inherently holy by morality, or outward works of piety? Or is it his intent to say that a sinner cannot attain to sanctification by his own strength, but that he must attain to it by the grace of God?

Take a survey of the chapter and follow the apostle's argumentation. All, both Jews and Gentiles, are under sin (verse 9); therefore every mouth must be stopped and none can plead innocence. All the world must be guilty before God, and so liable to condemnation (verse 19). What follows now? "Therefore by the works of the law shall no flesh be justified in His sight" (verse 20).

How strange would this conclusion be, taken in our adversaries' construction! They would take it to mean that by obedience unto the moral law done *without* grace, no flesh can attain sanctification in His sight. But neither does the apostle speak of sanctification but of absolution, as is apparent. All are sinners against the law; ergo, by pleading innocence in the keeping of the law, no man can be wholly sanctified, nor justified, nor absolved by blame in God's sight. Nor yet will the reason immediately annexed admit the gloss, "works without grace."

"By the works of the law shall no flesh be justified in His sight." Why not? "For by the law comes the knowledge of sin." That is, by the law men are convinced of sin and declared not to be innocent. This reason is not worth a rush, according to our adversaries' construction. He who without grace shall do the works of the law is not thereby made holy. Why? Because "by the law is the knowledge of sin." The law thus observed tells him he is a sinner, in which reason there is no force, unless it is true on the other side. Our opponents would say that he who by the help of grace does the works of the law is thereby sanctified, because the law thus tells him he is not a sinner—which is most untrue. Rather, not only those who are destitute of grace, but those who have grace also, and by the help thereof keep the law in some measure, are by the law, notwithstanding, shown to be sinners. The apostle yet goes on: if we are not justified by the works of the law, by what then? He answers in verse 21, "But now is the righteousness of God made manifest without the law." We are justified by the righteousness of God. But what is that? It is, says the distinction, that obedience to the law which we perform by God's grace. But this gloss is clearly false. For the righteousness of God here is a righteousness without the law; but obedience to the law, though performed with grace, is a righteousness *with* the law, because it is the righteousness *of* the law. For it is all one: he who obeys the law by his own strength, if he does it perfectly, as Adam, has the righteousness of the law. And he who obeys it perfectly, by God's grace, has still the same righteousness of the law and no other. For so the law is kept; it alters not the righteousness thereof whether we keep it by our own strength that we have of ourselves, or by another's help who gives us strength to do it. For then that strength which He gives us is our own. This point duly observed cuts asunder the sinews of this distinction. For it is clear that the apostle distinguishes the righteousness of the law and of God as different in their kinds. These make them to be one and the same thing, obedience to the moral law, but done by various helps—one by mere nature, the other by grace.

This is most contrary to the Scriptures, and especially to that excellent passage in Romans 10:5–11, where the apostle, showing the difference between the righteousness of God or faith, tells us that the righteousness of the law is thus described: "The man that doeth these things shall live thereby." But the righteousness of faith speaks in this way: "Whosoever believes on Him (i.e., Christ) shall not be ashamed." Can anything be more plain than that the apostle opposes here doing of the law and believing in Christ (versus not doing the law by our own strength and doing of the law by God's grace)? These are Jesuitical glosses that corrupt apostolic doctrine, and strangely pervert the work of Christ in our redemption, as if He had done no more for us but procured that, whereas we could not live by doing the law through our own strength, God will now aid us by His grace, that we may fulfill the law and by legal righteousness obtain justification and remission of sins.

We abhor such doctrine, and reject as vain and imaginary that distinction whence such absurdities necessarily follow. More might be said in confutation thereof, were it needful. But we have dwelt long upon this point, and it is time to hasten forward.

By the way, unto the Jesuit arguments in the defense of this distinction we answer:

1. We confess that faith is a work, and in doing it we obey the law because it is God's commandment that we believe in the name of His Son Jesus Christ (1 John 3:23). And therefore the gospel is called the law of faith because the promise of grace in Christ is propounded with the commandment that men believe it. But we deny that faith justifies us as a work which we perform in obedience to this law; it justifies us only as the condition required of us, and as an instrument of embracing Christ's righteousness. Nor can the contrary be proved.

2. The Jesuits are mistaken in the scope of the apostle, whose intent in Romans 3 is not to show that the Jews or Gentiles could not attain sanctification without God's grace by such obedience to the law as they could perform through the mere strength of natural abilities. They affirm it strongly, but their proofs are weak, being manifestly confuted by the whole file of the apostle's disputation, which clearly and plainly excludes both Jews and Gentiles from being justified by the works of the law without mak-

ing mention or giving the least intimation by what means these works must be performed, whether without grace or by the help of grace. Yea, it had been quite beside his purpose so to have done. For the apostle's argument is as clear as the light, and as strong as a threefold cord. All are sinners against the law; therefore, by obedience unto the law (let men perform it however they can, with or without grace), no man is in God's sight pronounced innocent.

3. To the last argument out of Romans 4:4 we answer that the apostle there proves that the faithful children of Abraham are not justified by works, because Abraham, the father of the faithful, was justified by faith and not by works. We affirm that the apostle excludes all the works of Abraham from his justification, both such as he performed when he had no grace and those he did when he had grace. For those works are excluded wherein Abraham might glory before men.

Now Abraham might glory before men as well—nay, even more—in those works which he did by the help of God's grace as those which he did without it: in his obedient departure from his own country at God's command, in his patient expectation of the promises, in his ready willingness even to offer his own son out of love and duty to God, in his religious behavior wherever he went. In those things Abraham had cause to glory before men, much more than in such works as he performed before his conversion when he served other gods.

Therefore we conclude that Abraham was justified neither by such works as went before faith and grace in him, nor yet by such as followed after. This is made most clear by the Romans 4:2: "If Abraham were justified by works, he had wherein to glory, but not with God." Admit here the popish interpretation and these words of the apostle will be false. Thus, if Abraham were justified by works, that is, by such works as he performed without God's gracious help, he has reason to glory before men, but not with God. Nay, that is quite otherwise, for it is evident that if a man is justified by obeying the law through his own strength, he may boldly glory before God as well as before men, seeing, in that case, that he is not beholden to God for His help.

But, according to our doctrine, the meaning of the apostle is perspicuous. Abraham might glory before men in those excellent works of piety which he performed after his vocation, and in men's sight he might be justified by them. But he could not glory in them before God, nor yet be justified by them in His sight. So then all works whatsoever are excluded from Abraham's justification, and nothing is left but faith, which is imputed unto him for righteousness, as it is in verse 3. Whence it follows that like Abraham, so all others are justified without all merit by God's free grace and favor. For so say verses 4–5: "Now unto him that works, the wages is not counted by favor, but by debt; but to him that works not, but believes in Him that justifies the ungodly, his faith is counted for righteousness."

These words ran clear till a Jesuit put his foot into the stream to raise up the mud. To him that works (that is, who fulfills the righteousness of the moral law) the wages of justification and life is not counted by favor, but by debt; for the perfect righteousness of the law a man deserves to be justified and saved. But to him who works not (who has not fulfilled the righteousness of the law in doing the law, in doing all things that are written therein, but believes in Him who justifies the ungodly—that is, relies upon Christ, who by His righteousness obtained abso-

Refuting Justification by other Graces

lution for him), that righteousness is in himself. His faith is imputed for righteousness; that is, he, by his faith, obtains justification in God's sight, not by merit of his own, but by God's gracious acceptance of Christ's righteousness as his.

But here our adversaries trouble the water by a false interpretation. "To him that works," they say, means him who fulfills the law by his own strength. Wages is not counted by favor, but by debt; but if he fulfills it by God's grace, his wages is paid him by favor, not of debt. Whereunto we reply:

1. This gloss is a plain corruption of the text. For by works in this fourth verse the apostle understands that kind of works whereof mention is made in verse 2, by which Abraham was not justified; and these, as we have shown, were works done by the help of grace, not by the mere strength of nature.

2. Again, as for the assertion itself, namely, that he who fulfills the moral law by the help of God's grace is justified by favor, not by debt, we say it is either a manifest falsehood, or at best an ambiguous speech. For it is one thing to bestow grace on a man to fulfill the law, and it is another thing to justify him when he has fulfilled the law. If God should give strength to a man exactly to fulfill the moral law, that would be indeed of His free favor and grace. But when this man who has received this strength shall come before God with the perfect righteousness of the law, pleading that in every point he had done what was required, God is bound in justice to pronounce him innocent and is in debt to bestow on him the wages of eternal life.

Adam's case is not unlike such a man. For God gave Adam what strength he had, yet Adam, fulfilling the law by that strength, should have merited justification and life. Therefore, when the apostle speaks of all works in the perfect fulfilling of the law, he says that, to him who works, wages are not counted by favor, but by debt. He speaks precisely, and the Jesuits, in excluding works done by grace, comment absurdly.

So much for the third point concerning man's justification by faith alone, as also for the first general heading promised at the beginning, namely, the condition required of us unto justification, which is faith.

SECTION III

Chapter 7

The righteousness whereby a man is justified before God is not his own or inherent in himself, and in this life no man has perfection of holiness inherent in him

I proceed unto the second general point in the matter of our justification, where we are to inquire what righteousness it is for which a sinner is justified in God's sight. Justification and justice are still coupled together, and there must be some righteousness for which God pronounces a man righteous, and for the sake whereof He forgives him all his sins. Nor is a sinner just before God because he is justified, but he is therefore justified because he is in some way or other just. The righteousness for which a man can be justified before God is of necessity one of these two: either he is inherently righteous in his own person and that righteousness is done by himself, or he is inherently righteous in the person of Christ, as that righteousness is imputed unto him.

A man is justified either by something *in* him and performed *by* him, or by something in another performed *for* him. The wisdom of angels and men has been unable to show unto us any third means. For it is affirmed by some that God might have reconciled mankind unto Himself by a free and absolute pardon of their sins without the intervention of any such righteousness either in themselves or in Christ whereby to procure it. To that we say that God has seen it to be good in this matter rather to follow His own most wise counsels than these men's foolish directions. It is to no purpose now to dispute what God *might* have done: whether God, by His absolute omnipotence, could not have freed men from hell by some other means without taking satisfaction for sin from Christ; whether God ought not to have the same privilege which we give unto any mortal king, freely to pardon a rebel and receive him to favor without consideration of any goodness in him, or satisfaction made by him, or by another for him; or whether sin makes such a deep wound in God's justice and honor that He cannot, with the safeguard of either, pass by it without amends. Such questions as these are vain and curious, prosecuted by idle and unthankful men who, not acknowledging the riches of God's wisdom and grace in that course of their redemption which God has followed, would accuse God of indiscretion, make much ado about nothing, and teach Him to have a more suitable way to work than by sending His own Son to die for us.

These criticisms of God's glorious and wonderful proceeding in man's redemption we leave unto Socinius and Arminius with their followers. It is our part to learn and obey—to understand what God has done, not to tell Him what He might or should have done. According to the course of His now-revealed will, we know that God has declared His everlasting hatred against sin, as that thing which most directly and immediately opposes the holiness of His nature and the justice of His commandments. We know that, because of this hatred which God bears to sin, no sinful creature could stand in His sight without being consumed with the fire of His fierce wrath. And therefore, before reconciliation, it was needful that satisfaction should be made where offense had been given. Seeing that man could not effect this by himself, God thought it good to provide a Mediator, who should make peace between both. So that whatever may be imagined of possibility of other means to bring man to life, yet now we know that it was thus necessary that Christ ought to suffer (Luke 24:26), and that it behooved Him to be like us, so that, being a faithful High Priest, He might make reconciliation for our sins (Hebrews 2:17).

Leaving then this new way to heaven, never frequented but by imagination, let us follow the old ways of justification that the Scriptures have revealed unto us, which are two and no more: we are justified either by our own righteousness and works or by the righteousness and works of another, Christ. The former is that way whereby man might have obtained justification and life had he not been a sinner; but now man, who is a sinner, cannot be justified and saved but only in the latter way, by the righteousness of Christ the Mediator.

This divine truth is of most infallible certainty and sovereign consolation unto the conscience of a sinner, as shall appear in the process of our discourse wherein we shall first remove our own righteousness so that, in the second place, we may establish the righteousness of Christ as the only matter of our justification in God's sight.

By "our own righteousness," we mean, as the apostle does in Romans 10, the righteousness of the law or the righteousness of works, which is twofold:

1. The fulfilling of the law, whether by the habitual holiness of the heart or by the actual justice of good works proceeding thence. For the law requires both that the

person be holy, endued with all inward qualities of purity and justice, and that the works be holy, being performed in substance and in any and all the circumstances according to the commandment.

2. The satisfying for the breach of the law. For he who makes full satisfaction to the law which is broken is afterward no debtor to the law, but is to be counted just and no violator thereof.

We must now inquire, regarding these two, whether a man can be justified by his own obedience to the moral law or whether he can be justified by his own satisfaction for transgression of the moral law. Concerning these two queries we lay down these two conclusions which are to be made good:

First, no man who is a sinner is justified by his own obedience to the moral law.

Second, no man is justified by his own satisfaction for his transgression.

As for the former, it is the conclusion of the apostle: "Therefore by the works of the law shall no flesh be justified in his sight" (Romans 3:20). This we prove by these arguments:

ARGUMENT 1. The first argument shall be that of the apostle in the aforenamed place, which proceeds as follows: whoever is a transgressor of the moral law cannot be justified by his obedience thereto. Every man is a transgressor of the moral law. Ergo, no man can be justified by his obedience thereto.

The first assertion of the syllogism is an undeniable principle in reason. It is impossible that a party accused as an offender should be absolved and pronounced innocent by pleading obedience to that law which he has plainly disobeyed. Wherefore the apostle takes this proposition

Justifying Righteousness is Not Inherent

for granted in these words of his: "For by the law comes the knowledge of sin" (Romans 3:20). That which shows us to be sinners cannot possibly declare us to be righteous. That plea will never acquit us which proves us guilty—yea, it would be not only folly, but madness to allege that as one's just excuse which itself is the very fault whereof he is accused. The major premise then is certain.

The minor premise is no less certain: that every man is a transgressor of the moral law. If any son of Adam will deny this, his own conscience will give his tongue the lie and the Scriptures will double it upon him, having "concluded all under sin" (Galatians 3:22). "If we (an apostle not excepted) say we have no sin we deceive ourselves and the truth is not in us. Yea, if we say we have not sinned, we make God a liar, and His word is not in us" (1 John 1:8, 10). The conclusion then is infallible that by the obedience of the moral law no man shall be justified, that is, acquitted and pronounced innocent before God's judgment seat. This apostolic argument utterly overthrows the pride of man in seeking justification by the law. And it is of such clear evidence that the adversaries of this doctrine cannot tell how to avoid it. But forasmuch as many exceptions are taken and shifts sought out, for the further manifestation of the force hereof against gainsayers of the truth, it will be requisite to examine their evasions. This we will do in the next argument:

ARGUMENT 2. Whosoever has once broken the law can never afterwards perfectly fulfill it. He cannot be justified by his obedience thereto. But now, having once broken God's law, man can never after that perfectly fulfill it. Ergo, man cannot be justified by his obedience to the law.

The major premise of this argument is framed upon no other ground than the first argument, and opposed unto that erroneous tenet of our adversaries who claim that however a man is a sinner against the law, yet, nevertheless, afterward he may be justified by his obedience to the law, because God for the time following gives him grace perfectly to fulfill it. This opinion is directly contrary to the reasoning of the apostle, which is that once a man is a sinner he is always incapable of justification by the law, for how should the law declare him innocent who has but once transgressed against it?

He who has stolen in his youth, and ever after lived truly and justly, can never acquit himself in judgment from guilt and punishment simply by pleading that he has kept the law in his latter times. Obedience that follows afterwards justifies not from the guilt that went before, as we shall see more hereafter in the point of man's satisfaction.

But let us grant that the law, though once broken yet afterwards fulfilled, would justify a man. We nevertheless defend the minor premise, that man having broken God's law can never afterwards perfectly fulfill it, and so by that means also he is excluded from justification by it. This proposition the Romanists will not yield to without strong proof. Let us explain and confirm it. The proposition may be set down in these terms: no man whosoever can perfectly fulfill the moral law in this life. Man here we consider in a twofold state—of nature and of grace. Regarding man in the estate of nature, it is agreed on both sides that the keeping of the law is utterly and absolutely impossible for him. But concerning man regenerate and justified, they of Rome affirm that he may keep the law. We of the Reformation grant that absolutely it is not impossible, for that we will not say. God might, if He saw fit, bestow such perfection of grace upon a regenerate man so that afterwards he should live without all sin and

Justifying Righteousness is Not Inherent

be translated to heaven without death. Yet according to the order which God now follows in bringing man to salvation, we deny that there ever was or ever will be any mortal man who has fulfilled or ever shall perfectly fulfill the righteousness of the moral law. This shall appear unto you by parting the righteousness of the law into its branches, whereby you may see what it is to fulfill the law and how impossible it is to do so.

The righteousness required by the moral law is of two sorts:

Habitual, in the inherent holiness of man's whole person, when such gracious qualities are fixed and planted in every faculty of soul and body as dispose and incline the motions of both only unto that which is conformable to the righteousness of the law. That such righteousness is required by the law is a plain case and confessed. That which commands the good or forbids the evil action commands the virtuous and forbids the vicious habit too. He who looks for purity in the stream cannot but dislike poison in the fountain. And God, who commands us to do good, bids us also to be holy. Nor can we do the one unless we do the other. And therefore the apostle joins both together. The end of the commandment is love—but where? Out of a pure heart (1 Timothy 1:5).

Actual, in the exercise of all good works enjoined by the law and forbearing the contrary evil works. This concept applies whether these good or evil works are *inward* in that spiritual obedience which the law requires (that is, in the right ordering of all the motions of our souls, so that every one of our thoughts, imaginations, purposes of our mind, and all the secret workings and stirrings of our affections, are altogether employed upon piety and charity, not so much as touching upon anything that is contrary to the love of God or our neighbor), or whether these good and evil works are *outward* in the bodily obedience unto the law, in doing all and every external duty of religion towards God, of justice and mercy towards man, and in leaving undone anything to the contrary.

Further, this actual righteousness of the law is to be considered in two ways:

First, as it respects all the commandments, and so only that righteousness is perfect which fulfills each and every particular precept of the law.

Second, as it respects any one commandment, or any one duty therein contained. And so we may call that righteousness perfect which exactly performs any one point of the law, though it fails in others.

So you see what is to be done by him who will perfectly fulfill the law. Let us now see whether or not any man can do so. We say no man can do it, and we make it good in the confirmation of three propositions:

1. No man in this life has perfection of grace and holiness inherently.

2. No man in this life can fully observe all those good works, both inward and outward, which the law requires.

3. No man in this life can perform any one particular good work so exactly that in every point it shall answer the rigor of the law and God's severe judgment.

As for the first, we prove it by this argument: where sinful corruption remains in part, there inherent holiness is not perfect. But in every man, during this life, there remains sinful corruption. Ergo, in no man is there, during this life, perfect, inherent holiness.

The major premise is without exception, for it is not possible that he who is in part bad and sinful should be totally good and holy.

The minor premise is most evident in Scripture, and in each man's experience and reason itself. The apostle describes corruption and grace in a regenerate man: "The flesh lusts against the Spirit, and the Spirit against the flesh; and these two are contrary one to the other, so that you cannot do the things that you would" (Galatians 5:17). Who can say that holiness is perfect in that man in whom corruption of nature not only troubles, but hinders grace in its holy operation? Shall we say this contention lasts but for a while after a man is newly regenerate, but that over time the Spirit gets an absolute victory, corruption being not only mastered, but annihilated? If we say so, experience will accuse us, and conscience will judge us to be liars.

Where is that man, and how is he named, who can say that he finds no rebellion or distemper in his affections or desires, no disorder in any motion of the soul, but that all within him is sweetly tuned unto obedience without jar and discord arising from corruption? Certainly that humble confession of a most holy Apostle may cause blushing in any such proud claimant. Had Paul the body of sin in him and you have none? He fights and wrestles against the law in his members, rebelling against the law of his mind, yea, he is so checked and mated by it that he can neither do the good he would nor avoid the evil he would not. When he would do well, evil was still present with him. And so tedious is this toil unto him that he complained of it at the very heart and cried out bitterly for help in this conflict. Whereupon, though he has help from God through Jesus Christ, yet he does not have full deliverance from this inherent corruption, but is fain to conclude in this pitiful manner: "So then I myself in my mind serve the law of God, but in my flesh the law of sin" (Romans 7:25).

Even Paul served God in the better half of him. Do what he can, sin will have place in his heart and a part of his service, though he is unwilling to yield it. If any will compare and prefer himself to this holy man, he may prove himself prouder, but better than him he cannot be.

It is arrogance for a simple friar to claim perfection when so great an apostle disavows it. If one will not acknowledge that corruption in himself which Paul (in the name of all) confessed in his own person, it is not because such a one is more holy than the apostle, but because he is ignorant and sees it not; or he is high-minded and scorns to be made aware of it.

Furthermore, reason confirms what Scripture and experience witness, that sinful corruption will hang fast upon us to our dying day. For if we suppose an utter abolishment of sin and corruption in our nature, it must follow that there will never be any sinfulness at all in our works and lives. Where the habit is perfect, the action is so too; and a sweet fountain cannot send forth bitter waters. Wherefore, seeing that the best of men cannot live without manifold actual sins, it is apparent that this ill fruit comes from a bad humor in the tree, and this defect of actual obedience comes from the imperfection of habitual holiness. This is sufficient for justification of the truth of our first proposition, that inherent holiness in this life is not perfect because it is always coupled with some sinful corruption.

But here our adversaries cry out with open mouth that we maintain a monstrous proposition, namely, that there is no inherent holiness in a man who is justified, that after justification a man still remains a sinner and unjust, that in justification sin is not abolished, but only covered with Christ's mantle. Thence they fall to their rhetoric that all

Justifying Righteousness is Not Inherent

Calvinists are but painted sepulchres, fair without and full of rottenness within. They say we are like foolish virgins who have no oil of their own, but think to be supplied by that of other folks; like wolves in a lamb's skin which hides, but does not take away, their ravening and fierce nature; like a leprous person in fine clothes who looks to be favored and embraced by his king because he is well appareled. For this is, they say, to teach that a man justified is yet a sinner in himself; that corruption, filthiness, and uncleanness remain in him when yet in God's sight he is accounted pure and clean because he has hidden himself under the cloak of Christ's righteousness. Whence also they tell us it will follow that we make Christ's body monstrous, a holy, beautiful Head joined to filthy, leprous members. Christ's marriage is hereby polluted, they say; you have a most holy and fair Bridegroom coupled to a foul, deformed spouse.

To this we say, "Truth is modest, yet you will not be outfaced with bigger words." Their eloquence has slandered partly us, partly the truth. They slander us in that they say we deny all inherent righteousness in a justified person, which is an impudent calumny. They slander the truth in condemning that as an error which is sacred verity taught us by God in the Scriptures, that a justified person is yet after that, in himself, in part sinful. This we still teach and maintain as a truth, firm as the foundation of the earth that cannot be shaken, namely that although a justified person is (by the grace of the Holy Ghost dwelling in him) made inherently holy, yet this sanctity is not that perfect purity of the heart which the law requires, because some degree of impurity and corruption dwells in him till death. And therefore the most justified person living is yet in himself partly sinful and unjust, but the sinfulness is pardoned unto him in Christ.

Against this the Romish contend, laboring to prove that in him who is justified sin does not remain at all, but is utterly abolished. They prove it by such arguments as these:

1. The Scriptures testify that Christ is the Lamb of God "that taketh away the sins of the world" (John 1:29); that He was offered to take away the sins of many (Hebrews 9:28); that in repentance our sins are blotted out (Acts 3:19); that God will subdue our iniquities and cast our sins into the bottom of the sea (in allusion to the drowning of the Egyptians in the Red Sea). Then surely it is abolished and remains no longer (Micah 7:19).

2. They prove it from the properties which are ascribed to sin. First, sin is compared to spots, stains, and filthiness; but from these we are washed by the pouring of clean water upon us, and by the blood of Christ (Ezekiel 16:25; 1 John 1:7; Revelation 1:6).

Second, sin is compared to bonds, fetters, and the prison, whereby we are held captive under the power of Satan. Now Christ has broken these chains and opened these prison doors, having delivered us from the power of darkness and redeemed us from all iniquity and made us free from sin to become the servants of righteousness (Romans 6:18, 22; Colossians 1:13; Titus 2:14).

Third, sin is compared to sicknesses, diseases, and wounds. Now God is the best Physician, the most skillful Surgeon, and where He undertakes the cure He does His work thoroughly. He cures all diseases and each one perfectly. He does not spread on a sick man a fair coverlet, or cover a festered wound with a fair cloth, as Calvin imagines, but by a purgative potion He expels the disease with a healing plaster. He cures the wound so that there re-

Justifying Righteousness is Not Inherent

mains no corrupt matter nor dangerous sore that can prove deadly. According to Romans 8:1, there is no condemnation to those who are in Christ Jesus. That is, there is no matter at all for which they deserve condemnation, as those expound.

Fourth, sin is likened to death, nay, the spiritual death of the soul. Now he who is justified is restored to spiritual life, and where life is there death is quite taken away, since a man cannot be both alive and dead at the same time. Wherefore the apostle says, "Our old man is crucified with Him, that the body of sin might be destroyed, that henceforth we might not serve sin" (Romans 6:6); "We are dead unto sin" (Romans 6:11).

Hence they conclude that if the filthiness of sin is washed away, the chains of sin broken, the diseases and hurts of sin healed, and the death of sin abolished, then it follows that sin is quite extinguished and remains no more in those who are justified.

3. They argue thus: If sin remains in those who are justified and are only covered, then God either knows of the sin or knows it not. To say He was ignorant of it would be blasphemy, all things being naked and bare before His eyes (Hebrews 4:14). If He knows it, then either He hates it or He hates it not. If He does not hate it, how do the Scriptures say truly that He is a God who hates iniquities? If He hates sin in them, then certainly He must punish it. God cannot see a fault and only hate it, but He must also punish it. If He punishes it, then he who is justified shall yet be condemned, which is absurd.

Unto these arguments we answer, first to the former two. When we say sin remains in a man who is regenerate and justified, we must distinguish the ambiguity of the word "sin." In sin, to use that distinction which is accepted by our adversaries, there are three things:

The offense of God, which is the fault.

The obligation unto eternal punishment, which is the guilt.

The stain or pollution of the soul, that is, the inherent vicious inclination of it unto evil. From this the fault committed first issued, and which by committing further faults it is augmented. For evil once committed leaves a further proneness in the heart to do it again. This we call the corruption of sin.

Thus we then answer that sin does not remain in those who are justified and regenerate in the two first respects, that is, of the fault and the guilt, both of which are taken away by the death of Christ. But sin does remain in the regenerate according to the third respect, that is, the vicious quality and corruption thereof which is inherent in the soul. We shall explain these answers, and apply them to the arguments.

We say then that the fault and guilt of sin in the regenerate are utterly abolished by the death of Christ. We do not thereby mean that in a regenerate man there is not one single fault or guilt to be found. For to say that when a regenerate man sins he is neither faulty nor guilty would be a gross untruth, as it is impossible that man should sin and yet God not be offended, or that man should sin and yet not be guilty and deserve eternal death. Wherefore we confess that in the holiest of men, if they sin, there is a true fault and God is displeased with it. There is also true guilt, and for it they deserve to go to hell.

But yet this truth also must be acknowledged by all, that all fault and guilt are quite abolished and taken away from them by Christ because both are pardoned unto them. God is offended, but yet they do not feel the woeful effects of His indignation because in Christ He is graciously contented to be reconciled with them. Again, they have deserved everlasting death, but they do not receive the pains thereof because they are freed from the punishment by Christ's satisfaction.

Thus, then, we understand the first part of the answer, that the fault and guilt of sin are utterly abolished, that is, totally pardoned unto the regenerate by means of Christ so that no final, eternal punishment shall befall them. The other part, that sin in its vicious quality and corruption remains in justified men, we understand with this necessary limitation: it remains in them not in its power and strength, but in its being and life (Romans 6:14, 21). It has life but not a kingdom. It reigns where there is no grace at all, but it lives even where grace is—which, though it mightily abates the power of it, cannot utterly destroy its being. Hence now it is easy to untie the arguments.

Sin is taken away, blotted out, and drowned in the bottom of the sea, in regard to those mischievous effects which sin would have brought on us. God is reconciled, the obligation to punish is canceled, and all the power, force, and strength of sin are defeated, so that like the dead Egyptians they can no longer pursue the Israelites to annoy them, nor shall they stand as an adversary in judgment to condemn us. The guilt of sin is washed away totally by the blood of Christ. The filthiness of corrupted nature is in part, by degrees, cleansed by the Spirit of Christ poured on us in His sanctifying grace. The fetters and bonds of sin whereby we were held in bondage under condemnation are quite broken asunder. But as for those chains whereby, with Paul, we are led captive to disobedience (Romans 7), some are broken and all weakened.

We are freed from the power of Satan and fear of hell,

though not wholly freed from sin, whereby we are often captives against our will. Sin is a sickness and God is the Physician; sin is a wound and God is the Surgeon. But He cures neither perfectly. Or, to state it more accurately, He cures our sickness and sores perfectly, but not suddenly. Where He begins the work He will finish it, but He will not do all in a day. The cure begins and goes onward to perfection during this life, but it is never finished till after death. He forgives all our iniquity, and that entirely and totally. He heals all our infirmities (Psalm 103:3), but this is by degrees, not all at once. In this course God has no cause to fear the censure of a Jesuit for unskillfulness, nor stands He in need of man's counsel for prescription, nor man's help to hold His hand in working if the cure goes on more slowly than our foolish hastiness thinks fit. That is fit and best which God thinks so, and if we count Him to be faithful and wise in His art, it is our duty to take His advice, but fancy presumption to give Him any.

Further, our adversaries argue that sin is the spiritual death of the soul, so where life is restored by justification, death must be quite abolished. The weakness of this argument appears clearly if the metaphorical terms are changed into proper ones. The death of sin is either the separation of all grace from the soul or the separation of God's favor from the soul. We are dead in trespasses and sins either way, in regard that in the unregenerate state the soul is utterly destitute of all grace and goodness, and also because in that condition it is liable to eternal death. Now the death of sin that is eternal death in the perpetual loss of God's favor is fully taken away from him who is regenerate. Christ by His death has purchased for him life and immortality. But regarding that other death, that is, the want of all inherent grace in the soul, we say that in regeneration, grace and holiness are restored to the soul, yet not so perfectly as to abolish every degree of sinful corruption. Before regeneration the soul had no grace at all and so was utterly dead, but it does not follow that therefore, in regeneration, it has all grace given to it in all perfection, and so is made perfectly alive.

Whatever harshness there is in the metaphor, the plain terms in this case are smooth enough. A man may be at once alive and dead, that is, at once a man may be partly holy and partly sinful. Our old man is crucified with Christ upon whose cross it received a deadly wound, because Christ by His sacrifice has procured the sending of the Holy Ghost into the hearts of the elect. By sanctifying them, He abolished their natural corruptions by degrees, so that the body of sin might be destroyed that is not presently annihilated. Sin has been made of no force and strength, made unable to work strongly in us, that henceforth we might not serve sin, though always we will have sin in us. So we are dead to sin, not as if sin were utterly dead in us, or had no more working in us than it has in a dead carcass, but because the guilt of sin is fully taken away, and the power of sin has received a deadly wound; it bleeds out some of its life now, and shall infallibly bleed out the last drop of its life hereafter.

Unto the third argument we answer that the horns of those dilemmas are made of wood and may be easily battered. We grant that God sees and knows the sinful corruption which is in the regenerate. For we cannot assent unto that wild and frantic imagination of some who have troubled the quiet of some places in this land by preaching that God does not, nay, cannot see any iniquity or matter of blame in those who are in Christ Jesus. We believe that nothing is hidden from His eyes, nor are our sins less visible to Him than our graces.

God knows what sins His children commit. He judges them to be faults, and such as deserve His infinite wrath. Yea, to go further, as He sees the sin of the regenerate, so He hates it with a perfect hatred, it being impossible that His pure eyes should behold impurity and love it. But now what follows hence? If He sees it and hates it, then He cannot but punish it. True, that consequence is certain. But what is next? If God punishes that sin which is in the regenerate, how then is their sin covered and their iniquities forgiven? How does He account them to be just whom He knows and punishes as unjust? Here is the sophism: He sees sin, hates sin, and punishes sin in the regenerate. Therefore He punishes it in and upon their own persons. But that is a *non sequitur*. He punishes it, but it is in the person of Christ who has trodden the winepress of the fierce wrath of God conceived against all sinfulness whatsoever in His elect. By this means His hatred towards the sin of the regenerate is fully satisfied, and also His love toward their persons is procured. He graciously passes by their iniquity, pardoning unto them what He hates and has punished in Christ, in which respect He may be truly said not to see that sin in them which He will never punish in them, and to cover that sin which shall never be laid open in judgment against them.

Chapter 8

No man can perfectly fulfill the law in performing all such works, both inward and outward, as each commandment requires, against which truth popish objections are answered

We go on unto the next proposition concerning man's actual obedience unto the whole law. We teach that no man can perfectly obey the law in performing all such works, both inward and outward, as each commandment requires.

A man would think this point needed no other proof but experience. In all the catalog of the saints, can you pick out one who, after regeneration, never committed sin against the law? We shall kiss the ground he treaded on if we know where that man haunts who can assure us that since his conversion he never broke the law. Shall we find this perfection in a monk's cell, in a hermit's lodge, an Anchorite's mule, under a cardinal's hat, or in the pope's chair? All these are cages of uncleanness, not temples wherein dwells undefiled sanctity.

Never to sin is a happiness of saints and angels with whom we shall hereafter enjoy it; but while we are mortal we can but wish for it. "Thy law," said David, "is exceeding large" (Psalm 119:96). It comprises in it not a few, but many and manifold duties. Good works are, by a kind of popish solecism, brought to a short sum: prayer, fasting, and alms deeds. These are eminent among the rest, but not the hundredth part of the whole number. There is besides a world of duties enjoined and as many sins forbidden. Each commandment has its several ranks, every duty its manifold circumstances; to reckon up all would be a business which the wit of the subtlest Jesuit or the profoundest divine could hardly master. To perform them is a task which is beyond the strength of the holiest man, who in finding it a great difficulty to do any one well would forthwith judge the performance of so many to be an impossibility. But if this suffices not, we have express Scriptures to prove that no man actually obeys the law in all points. Such places are these: "There is no man that sins not" (1 Kings 8:46). "For there is not a just man upon the earth that does good and sins not" (Ecclesiastes 7:20). "In many things we offend all" (James 3:2). "If we say that we have no sin, we deceive ourselves and the truth is not in us" (1 John 1:8).

Hence we conclude that in fact no one ever fully keeps the law, but we all break it in some, yea, in many things. And therefore we say that the dispute of our adversaries, regarding the possibility of keeping the law, vanishes into nothing. For since no man ever has or will actually keep it (as the Scriptures witness), to what end are all the quarreling and disputes about the possibility of keeping it? No man shall be justified by the law because he has a power to keep it if he will, but because he has actually kept it.

Hence it is manifest that the reply of our adversaries is ridiculous: "No man indeed keeps it, but yet they may if they will." For what is that to justification? Can a man who is regenerate be justified by his obedience of the law, when yet after his regeneration he does not keep it? Again, how do these men know that there was or is such a power in the saints to keep the law when yet the world never saw it brought into action? Is it not more probable that what never was nor will be done never could nor can be done? Were they all idle and did not do their best endeavor? It is true that none does so much good as he should and might, but yet it is a sharp censure to say that none would put themselves forward to the utmost of their might.

What shall be said of St. Paul? He confessed that he was not yet perfect, but that he sought after it (Philippians 3:12). How? Negligently? No, with great diligence and intention. He followed after righteousness, and that eagerly, reaching forth to catch the things that were before him, pressing towards the mark (Philippians 3:13–14). Here was diligence, and we cannot say that St. Paul did not do his best. Did Paul then fulfill the law? It seems so, for here we see he was willing. And, in another place, Bellarmine tells us Paul was able, for so we have it: "I can do all things through Christ which strengtheneth me" (Philippians 4:13), that is, "I can fulfill the moral law by the grace of Christ." Now if he were willing and able, then certainly he kept it, the papists say.

Nay, it is certain that he did *not* keep it. Witness his own testimony: "I do not the good things which I would; but the evil which I would not, that I do" (Romans 7:19). Where is the fault, then? In the apostle's will? No, it is plain that he would have done it. Was it then in his ability? Yea, this was it. To will was present with him, but he found no means to perform that which is good (Romans 7:18).

The Jesuit then abuses us with a false exposition of that passage in Philippians, interpreting it as referring to the apostle's ability to perform the moral law, when he was clearly speaking of that strength wherewith Christ enabled him to have contentment and patience in all conditions whatsoever. Paul was able to bear all afflictions patiently and to use prosperity soberly; but to fulfill the law in all things perfectly he was not able. And if *he* was not able, who is? We conclude that the actual obedience of the moral law in fulfilling all the commandments exactly is impossible for a regenerate man in this life.

Let us now take a short survey of our adversaries' arguments whereby they would prove that actual obedience to the whole law is not only possible, but also very easy for the regenerate and justified:

ARGUMENT 1. That burden which is light may be carried without shrinking under it; that yoke which is easy is worn without pain. Those commandments which are not burdensome may be observed without difficulty. But such is the moral law. "My yoke is easy and My burden is light" (Matthew 11:30). "This is the love of God, that you keep His commandments; and His commandments are not grievous" (1 John 5:3). Ergo, the moral law may be easily observed.

To this we answer that the verse in Matthew is to be understood not of the moral law, but of the yoke and burden of the cross and afflictions which everyone must bear who will follow Christ and obey the gospel. To those who are wearied and laden with the cross, Christ speaks by way of consolation, telling them where to resort for help. "Come to Me and I will give you rest," that is, comfort and deliverance. Then He persuades them to have patience in their affliction: "Take My yoke upon you and bear it cheerfully," which persuasion He strengthens with three arguments:

First, from His own example: "Learn of Me. Do and suffer as I do, enduring so many persecutions and afflic-

No Man Can Perfectly Fulfill the Law

tions with all meekness and patience. For I am meek and lowly in heart, quietly bearing all wrongs and indignities from man without murmuring against God, repining against man, or seeking revenge at the hands of those who have unjustly persecuted Me."

Second, from the success of this patient enduring according to Christ's example: "And you shall find rest unto your souls," comfort in affliction, seasonable deliverance from affliction.

Third, from the nature of such crosses: "For My yoke is easy and My burden is light." Though they are yokes and burdens which for the present seem grievous, yet they are easy. They are light, because they are Christ's yoke and Christ's burden, which He lays on all His true disciples who follow Him, and which He will give them strength to bear with cheerfulness.

This seems the most natural interpretation of this place, and it is most agreeable to Hebrews 12 where the like arguments are used to comfort the godly in such afflictions as follow the profession of the gospel. But if we understand it as referring to the yoke and burden of the law, we answer, relying on 1 John 5:3, that the reason why the commandments of God are not grievous to the regenerate is not because they can perfectly and easily fulfill them, but because that which made them intolerable and insupportable is now taken away. What is that? The rigor of the law in requiring of every man exact obedience under the pain of the curse of eternal death. Here was the uneasiness of the yoke which pinched man in his sinful state. This was the weight of the burden under which every man outside of Christ must be crushed and sink down to hell. Now Christ, having fulfilled the law and made satisfaction for all our transgressions thereof, has made this yoke easy for the necks, and has made this burden light upon the shoulders of the regenerate, because, though they are called to obey, yet it is not upon those severe terms of being eternally accursed if they at any time disobey. Now they are assured that their hearty obedience shall be accepted so far as they are able to perform it, and where they fail they shall be mercifully pardoned. This is a singular encouragement to a Christian's heart that he might show all willing and cheerful endeavor in obeying God's commandments, whereby he may give good proof of his unfeigned love unto God.

Again we answer that this uneasy and burdensome nature of the moral law is to be taken in regard to the enmity and opposition which a carnal man bears unto the obedience thereof. Unto a natural man it is the greatest toil and wearisomeness in the world for him to be made to draw in this yoke. For him to bridle his desires, to check his disordered affections, to restrain himself from his pleasures, to be tied to the exercise of religion, to have a lawless mind brought in subjection to a strict law—oh, what a weariness it is, how he grumbles at it! He chafes and sweats under such a burden, more than under the weight of ten talents of lead.

But now unto a heart sanctified by grace, all such obedience becomes sweet, pleasant, and delightful. The heart now loves the holiness of the law. It delights in the law (Romans 7:22), takes contentment in obeying it (Psalm 119), and is full of singular affection and desire after it. Whence, though it fails in many things through manifold infirmities and temptations, yet it ceases not in a willing, constant, and cheerful endeavor to perform all. Grace fights with many difficulties, and in the combat takes many a foil; but yet at last the victory falls on her side. For, says Saint John, "he that is born of God overcomes the world" (1 John 5:4). Thus "the lust of the eyes, the lust of the flesh, and the pride of life," by which he means the temptations of this world (1 John 2:16), prevail not against him to turn him away from the holy commandment given unto him. But he still obeys cheerfully and sincerely, though not every way perfectly. This responds to the first argument.

ARGUMENT 2. If the hardest precepts of the law may be kept, then much more all the rest which are easier. But the hardest precepts may be observed. Ergo, the rest also.

They prove the minor premise thus: Three precepts are the hardest, which all confess:

You shall love the Lord with all your heart.

You shall love your neighbor as yourself.

You shall not covet—the tenth commandment.

But now all these three commandments may be kept by the regenerate; ergo, they can keep the rest, and so the whole law.

We deny the minor premise of the syllogism, and say that those three precepts are not kept perfectly by any man in this life. Let us discuss how they approach each particular.

(1) That a man in this life may love God with his whole heart. This they prove:

First, by Scripture. "The Lord thy God will circumcise thy heart, and the heart of the seed, to love the Lord thy God with all thy heart, and with all thy soul, that thou mayest live" (Deuteronomy 30:6). This is a prediction or promise of that which was heretofore and is still accomplished in the regenerate, who, being sanctified and purified from sin (a work of God's Spirit in the heart symbolized by external circumcision of the flesh), should love

God with all their hearts.

Second, by the example of David, who says of himself, "With my whole heart have I sought Thee" (Psalm 119:10). And God also testifies of him that he kept His commandments, and followed Him with all his heart, to do that only which was righteous in His eyes (1 Kings 14:8). The like is recorded of Josiah, and "like unto him was there no king before him that turned to the Lord with all his heart, and with all his soul, and with all his might according to all the law of Moses; neither after him arose any like him" (2 Kings 23:25). These men, then, loved God with all their hearts.

Third, by reason, for to love God with all the heart carries one of these three senses. First, it could mean to love Him only and nothing else, and so we are not commanded to love God with all our heart because we must love our neighbor too. Second, to love Him with as much effort as can be made, that is, as much as may be. Nor is this commanded, says Becanus, and yet if it were, who would say it is impossible to love God as much as one can? Third, to love God above all, that is, to prefer Him before all creatures, before father and mother, as Christ bids (Matthew 10:37), and as Abraham did before his only son. Now this only is to love God with all the heart, and this men may do, as appears in the martyrs and others who left all for God's love.

Unto this argument we answer that it is not so easy a matter to love God with all the heart as these imagine. Bellarmine indeed includes a "but" in it. There is nothing required of us, he says, "but" to love God with all the heart, as if it were as easily done as spoken. But we believe that in this "but" God has set up a target which all the men in the world may and must aim at, yet none will shoot so steadily as to hit it. Regarding the passage cited in Deuteronomy, we say that God therein tells us what His gracious work is in circumcising or sanctifying our hearts, and what our bound duty is thereupon, that is, to love Him with all our hearts, the performance whereof we must endeavor sincerely, though we cannot do it perfectly.

With regard to the examples of David and Josiah, who are said to follow the Lord with all their heart, nothing else is meant thereby but a sincere intent and endeavor in general to establish and maintain God's pure religion in their kingdom free from corruption of idolatry, as well as their own particular blameless conduct. In David's case, it is clear that not perfection, but sincerity is his commendation, as his many sins recorded in the Scriptures witness sufficiently that he had in his heart that corruption which many times turned the love thereof from God to other things. How did he love God with all his heart when he defiled Uriah's bed, shed Uriah's blood, intended to murder Nabal, or judged away an honest man's lands to a fawning sycophant, along with other such faults? The prophet himself in that place witnesses as to the uprightness of his heart. "With my whole heart have I sought Thee" (Psalm 119:10). He does so with all the weakness and corruption of it, against which he humbly craves God's assistance in the very next words: "Let me not wander from Thy commandments."

As for Josiah, it is plain that this singular commendation is given to him because of his thorough reformations of the most corrupt estate of religion which prevailed before his reign, wherein many godly kings before him had done something in redressing some abuses, but none went so far in a zealous reformation of all, according to Moses' law. Wherefore the text says that there was no king before him like him, which cannot be meant absolutely of all, for David is said to have followed God's will with all his heart as well as Josiah; but since the time when religion began to be corrupted in the Jewish church, there was none of all the kings of Judah who was so faithful as Josiah to restore all things to the first purity. Whence he has the praise that he turned unto God more entirely than any other king before or after him. But now, to conclude based on Josiah's zeal in reformation that in every particular of his life he kept the law perfectly, loving God with all his heart, is a consequence that lacks strength of connection.

Unto the argument from reason based on the meaning of the law we grant that the first option is not the meaning of it; but we do not discuss the second, that is, that to love God with all the heart is to love Him as much as may be. The Jesuit has no reason either to deny that this is commanded or to affirm that if it were commanded it is yet possible to do it.

Would any man say, unless he cares not what he says, that God does not command us to love Him as much as may be? Or will it be a truth from any man's tongue to say that he loves God with as great perfection as may be? It cannot, which appears thus: God's will is that we should love Him with all our hearts. Now Christ has taught us to pray, "Thy will be done in earth as it is in heaven." Thence it is evident that we on earth are bound to fulfill the commandment of loving God as the saints in heaven do fulfill it. But now our adversaries themselves grant that while we may be on the way, we cannot love God so much as we shall do in the fatherland. Whence it follows that no man can love Him so much as may be and as he ought to do. So no man has his heart replenished with that measure of divine love whereof his nature is capable, which either Adam had in his innocence or the saints have in glory.

As for the third possible interpretation of the words, we grant indeed that to love God with all the heart is to love Him above all creatures. But the Jesuits take here but one part of true love of God. It is a singular part of divine love when the heart is so fixed on God that neither the love nor fear of any earthly thing can draw it away from obeying God. This, we say, is a matter wherein everyone fails in some way or another, more or less, though in the end many martyrs and other holy men have herein by faith overcome the world. But to prefer God before all temporal pains and pleasure, profits or discommodities, does not by itself constitute perfect love. He loves God with all his heart not only who loves Him above all, but also who obeys God in all. "This is the love of God, that we keep His commandments." He who, though claiming to love God, will not obey God's law loves his sins more than God. Offend but in the least thing, and there is presently want of love; for he who will not do as God bids him is, at that point, void of that love which moves him to obey at other times. He then who keeps God's Word, in him is the love of God perfect indeed (1 John 2:5). Perfect obedience and perfect love are inseparable. Now as the former cannot be found in moral men, we cannot seek in them for the latter. And therefore this commandment ("Love God above all things") cannot be kept in this life.

(2) That a man may love his neighbor as himself. For this purpose they turn us to Romans 13:8–10: "He that loves another has fulfilled the law, because the law is comprehended in this saying, Thou shalt love thy neighbor as thyself. And love does no evil to his neighbor; therefore is love the fulfilling of the law." And they bid us

look where we read, "For all the law is fulfilled in one word, Thou shalt love thy neighbor as thyself" (Galatians 5:14).

Hereto we answer that there is in these places nothing that needs answering. We grant that the love of our neighbor as ourselves is the fulfilling of the law, that is, of the second table of the law regarding our duty unto man; and so much these places witness, commanding us also so to do. But now how do our adversaries prove out of these places that men can perfectly observe this law? We agree that the regenerate love their neighbors as themselves—but with that perfection of love which in every point fulfills the law, doing our neighbor no hurt but all good, and in all our thoughts, words, and deed? This we cannot grant them unless it is upon better proofs.

(3) Let us go to the Tenth Commandment which they say may be kept, that is, "Thou shalt not covet." This tenth commandment of the Decalogue is, they say, possible to be fulfilled by a regenerate man. For three things must be observed concerning this concupiscence or coveting forbidden in the Tenth Commandment:

First, the vicious proneness and inclination of nature unto bad desires, which is called concupiscence in its initial stage, such as when one has a thievish mind.

Second, the inordinate motions of the heart immediately arising from that corrupt disposition which prevents reason and goes before consent (such as when one desires another man's money) but which suddenly vanishes of itself, or upon deliberation it is checked.

Third, the consent of the will, either when it takes immediate delight in such desires themselves, as in speculative fornication, or when it resolves to put in execution what the heart imagined, as to lay a plot to despoil another of his goods.

The two former, the vicious disposition of nature and inordinate desire that goes before consent, are no sins, say the Romanists, and so are not forbidden in the Ten Commandments. The last, evil desires with consent, are the very sins which are forbidden in that commandment. Whence they conclude that a regenerate man may avoid the breach of this commandment, for it is in the power of his will whether he will consent unto such motions of the heart or not; and if he does not consent, then he sins not.

Hereunto we answer that when they of Rome teach that the habitual viciousness of nature and the disorderly motions of the heart which go before consent are not sins, they therein err grossly against Scripture and sound reason. It is the gift of these men always to judge flatteringly and favorably on nature's side. They conceive in themselves a God in heaven like their god in Rome, an easy god. As a result they will wink at small faults and grant indulgences by the dozen. And look what they judge a small matter: God must be of their mind or else they are not pleased. His love must fit their concept of what they think they can do; that God shall have leave to command or forbid. But, if otherwise, they will tell Him to His face that He is a fool or a tyrant to command them that which now they cannot perform. For God, they say, to require of man a freedom from all vicious inclinations and evil desires would be as mad an injunction as for a master to command his servant never to be hungry or thirsty, hot or cold, and to threaten him that he should look through a halter in case it be otherwise with him.

This error we shall more conveniently speak of in the refutation of common and general objections which they make against all those proofs that demonstrate the impossibility of keeping the law, whereof this is one, that concupiscence in the first and second form is not sin. But now whereas they affirm that it is in a regenerate man's power not to yield consent to the motion of sin, and that therefore he may fulfill the law which said, "Thou shalt not lust," we grant then that the Spirit may many times get the victory, overmastering such unruly motions of the heart. But this is not perpetual, for there is nobody (except those extremely ignorant of grace and nature) but will confess that many times these affections for sins, as the apostle calls them, work in them so strongly, upon such circumstances and advantages, that they do not only combat and fight against the powers of grace, but also vanquish them, and even lead a regenerate man captive unto the law or command of sin. The apostle confesses so much of himself (Romans 7:23), even though he was able to do as much as he who thinks himself best. And therefore, whatever power we may seem to have not to yield consent, yet it is certain that we shall often fail in our practice. So much for the second argument touching on the observation of the hardest precepts of the law.

ARGUMENT 3. If a man may do more than the law requires, he may certainly do as much. But a man may do more than the law requires. Ergo, he may do as much. The minor premise Bellarmine proves by the example of the young man who told Christ that he had observed all the commandments from his youth. Our Savior bade him do one thing more, and then he would be perfect: "If you would be perfect, go sell all that you have, and give to the poor, and follow Me" (Matthew 19:21). Now if the young man had done this, he would have done more than the law required, inasmuch as whatsoever the law required he had observed formerly. For do you not believe that he

No Man Can Perfectly Fulfill the Law

spoke truly when he said, "All these things I have observed from my youth"?

We answer that we do not believe the testimony of that vain young man concerning his own righteousness, who boasted of keeping the second table in the outward duties thereof when as yet he lacked inward charity towards his neighbor and love towards God. He vouchsafed that he had kept all these duties perfectly, fulfilling that commandment, "Thou shalt love thy neighbor as thyself," and thereupon was so bold as to ask Christ, "What do I lack yet?"

Christ, to convince him of his pride and wants, put him to the trial: "If you have such perfect charity towards man, then, certainly, if God commands you to bestow not a part, but all of your goods upon the poor upon promise of better things to yourself, your duty to God and singular charity to men will make you do so. Go, then, sell all that you have and give to the poor." Upon this special commandment, this covetous mind showed itself. Nay, it is plain that he did not love his neighbor as well as his riches. He is neither so dutiful to God nor charitable to the poor as, for either of their sakes, to part with his possessions.

"But," might he say, "what? Will not ordinary alms, or a little more than ordinary, serve the turn? Must I give away all? Indeed the law requires that I be merciful to the poor, but where is any law that bids me sell my whole estate and distribute to them who want? Christ lays an unnecessary burden upon me. If I cannot be perfect without undoing myself, I will content myself as I am and not seek after such perfection."

Here a papist will say he spoke reason, since Christ's speech was but a counsel of more perfection than the law required. Now a man is not to be blamed if he chooses only to be as perfect as the law commands him, and so this young man was, if you will believe him or them.

But the Scripture makes it plain that he did evil in disobeying Christ, and that if he had obeyed Him in that particular he would have done no more than the law required at his hands. For obedience to every special commandment is included in the general. The law indefinitely commands us to give alms. Now if God, by a special commandment, limits how much we shall give, whether half or all our estates, to obey such a particular precept is not to do more than the general law requires of us. Such a particular commandment was this one of Christ unto the young man, wherein He challenged him, according to that concept of perfection which he had of himself, putting him to the practice of the highest duty which the law of liberality can possibly require of a man, to part with all. This he ought to have done upon Christ's particular commandment. In not doing it he broke the law and proclaimed his heart to be full of covetousness, devoid of faith in God and true charity towards his neighbor.

From this passage, then, our adversaries cannot prove that this young man might have done more than the law required, or that we are bound at any time to do as Christ bade him. Christ's command was for his particular trial, not for our imitation. They who take it otherwise are a generation of men who profess beggary and possess kingdoms, who were willing enough to part with what little they had of their own that they may live the more comfortably and plentifully upon other men's. We go forward to the next argument.

ARGUMENT 4. If the law were impossible to be kept it would be no law, for there is no law of things that are im-

No Man Can Perfectly Fulfill the Law

possible. Yea, God would be more cruel and foolish than any tyrant to command us to do what is impossible for us to do.

To this we answer that the consequences would be true if God had given a law which men never had strength to perform. But now the law written in tables on Mount Sinai was but a reviving and repetition of the same law which was written in Adam's heart, the characters whereof were now defaced in his sinful posterity. Adam had strength sufficient to fulfill it; as he received for himself and us so he lost it for both. Nevertheless, though strength to obey is lost, yet the obligation to obey remains. We are no more discharged of our duties because we have no strength to do it than a debtor is acquitted of his debts because he lacks money to make payment. Nor is this cruelty or folly in God that when He published this law unto the Israelites He did not qualify the exactness thereof, fitting the precepts to their abilities, commanding them to do just as much as they could or would do. Had God made a law of that sort in favor of man's sinful nature, they might with better reason have laid folly to His charge for bending the rule to the crookedness of man's heart, and not leveling it according to the straightness of the rule. God was to set forth a law of liberty that should not flatter, but should freely rebuke man of all unrighteousness—a perfect law containing in it a full description of holiness and justice which man ought to have and perform towards God and his neighbor (James 1:25; Psalm 19:7). In this case God has just reason to have respect unto man's duty, not his ability which he once had but now has forfeited and lost.

ARGUMENT 5. Every prayer made in faith according to God's will is heard and granted. But we pray that we may fulfill the law perfectly (for we pray that we may do

God's will in earth, as it is in heaven). Ergo, God hears us and gives us such grace that we can do it.

Hereto we answer that this prayer shows us what we are bound to, and what is our duty continually to endeavor: that we may do God's will every day more perfectly, cheerfully, and constantly than before. And so far God hears the faithful prayers of His loving children, enabling them to better perform their obedience. That this is given to us in this life, as the saints enjoy it in heaven, will not be granted by our adversaries themselves. Wherefore they must also grant that that prayer is heard and granted to us by degrees. In this life we attain such perfection as God sees fit for us; afterwards He gives us that which is complete.

ARGUMENT 6. They attempt to prove by the following Scriptures that the law may be fulfilled. The apostle reckons up the fruit of the Spirit: love, joy, peace, and others. Then he says that "against such there is no law" (Galatians 5:23). That is, says Bellarmine, the law cannot accuse such men of sin. So, "whosoever is born of God does not commit sin, for His seed remains in him; and he cannot sin, because he is born of God" (1 John 3:9). Ergo, the regenerate cannot so much as break the law.

We answer that both these places are perverted by false interpretations. "Against such there is no law," says the apostle. Against what? Such persons, or such graces? If it is meant of persons, such as have the Spirit and bring forth the fruit of the Spirit there mentioned, then, again there is no law. But we must take it in the apostle's own meaning, which he expresses: "If you be led by the Spirit, you are not under the law" (Galatians 5:18). How is that? Are not the regenerate under the law, that is, under the obedience of the law? Yes, we grant on both sides that grace does not free us from subjection and obedience unto God's law. How then are they not under the law?

It is plain. They are not under the curse and condemnation of the law as those are who walk in the flesh and do the works thereof, who therefore shall not inherit the kingdom of God (Galatians 5:19), and who will be accursed. But such as walk in the Spirit, being regenerate and justified, are not under the curse. Therefore, though the law may and does accuse them of sin, yet the law is not so against them as to bring condemnation upon them as it does upon others, from which in Christ they are freed.

If the clause is understood of the graces of the Spirit there reckoned up, the sense is this: Against such works there is no law forbidding them, as there is against works of the flesh; these are agreeable to the law, while those are contrary to the law. But this does not help our adversaries' purpose. For 1 John 3:9 says, "He that is born of God does not commit sin, yea, cannot." If our adversaries' exposition according to the very letter may stand good, it will follow that in the regenerate there is not only a possibility of keeping the law, but also an impossibility at any time of breaking it. But they easily see how absurd this position is, and that if it were granted, their doctrine of falling away from grace would lie flat in the dust, since John says expressly that a regenerate man not only does not, but *cannot* sin. Therefore certainly he cannot fall from grace.

They help it out with this distinction: He cannot sin, that is, mortally. He may sin venially, and venial sins may stand with grace and with perfect obedience of the law. This distinction is one of the rotten pillars of the Romish Church. It will come in a fit place to be examined hereafter; for the present we say he who sins venially (as they mince it) breaks the law. And again, a regenerate man may sin mortally, which is true not only according to their doctrine, since they teach that a man may fall from the grace of regeneration and that to do so is a mortal sin, but much more according to the Scriptures and experience, which witness that Peter, David, Solomon, and many, yea, all the saints have had at some time or another their grievous falls, out of which, notwithstanding by the grace of the Holy Ghost abiding in them, they recover themselves so that finally they fall not away.

ARGUMENT 7. The last argument is from the examples of such men as have fulfilled the law. The Scriptures record that various men have been perfect in fulfilling the law in all things, such as Abraham (Genesis 17:1), Noah (Genesis 6:9), David (1 Kings 14:8), Josiah (2 Kings 23:25), Asa (2 Chronicles 25:17), Zechariah and Elizabeth (Luke 1:6), the apostles (John 17:6), and other holy men (Philippians 3:15). Therefore the law is at least possible to be kept by some.

Not making particular examination of all the passages of Scripture which are alleged for proof of these examples, we answer briefly. It is every man's duty to aim at perfection in his obedience, according to Christ's commandment: "Be ye therefore perfect even as your Father in heaven is perfect" (Matthew 5:48). In this life there are many degrees of grace, which God bestows diversely on various men according to His own pleasure and their greater or lesser diligence in the practice of holiness. So that, comparatively, some men may be said to be perfect because they are far more perfect than others. Likewise, the greatest stars are said to be of perfect light because they shine more brightly than those of lesser magnitude, though yet not so brightly as the sun.

But we affirm that no man in this endeavor after perfection goes so far, as for inward holiness and outward obedience, as to answer the perfection of the law in all points. Even in these holy saints whom they cite as examples, the Scriptures have recorded for us their failings so that in them at once we may see a pattern of holiness to be imitated and an example of human infirmity to be admonished by. We have Abraham sometimes doubting God's promise and protection (Genesis 15:2–3), and helping himself by a shift that was scarcely warranted (Genesis 20:11–13). Noah was overcome by drinks (Genesis 9:21). David broke the sixth and seventh commandments one after another (2 Samuel 11). Josiah ran willfully upon a dangerous enterprise against God's commandment (2 Chronicles 25). Asa relied on the king of Syria for help against the king of Israel, and not upon the Lord, and in a rage imprisoned the prophets for reproving him, and in his disease sought not the Lord, but the physicians (2 Chronicles 16:7–12). Zechariah did not give credence to the angel's message (Luke 1:18), and the apostles all at a clap forsook or denied Christ (Mark 14:50, 66–71). We cannot then in these saints find perfection in the full obedience to the law; among whose few actions registered by the Holy Ghost's pen, we may read their sins together with their good works. And had the Scriptures been silent in that point, yet who could thence have concluded that these men or others had no faults because no mention is made of them? It was God's purpose to relate the most eminent events, not every particular action of their lives. Even Christ's story falls short of such exactness (John 20:30–31).

We conclude then, notwithstanding these arguments, that our second proposition stands firm and good, that no man in this life can fulfill the law in every duty both inward and outward, but that the most just man on earth will fail in many things. So if he should seek for justification by his actual obedience to the law, he throws himself under the curse of the law. For "cursed is every one that continues not in all things, which are written in the book of the law to do them," said the apostle (Galatians 3:10), quoting Moses (Deuteronomy 27:26). This curse must fall on those who are of the works of the law, that is, who seek for justification and life by the obedience of the law, which yet they cannot in all things perfectly obey.

Chapter 9

No man in this life can perform any particular good work so exactly that in every point it shall answer the rigor of the law, proved by conscience, Scriptures, and reason. Also, popish objections are answered.

I proceed unto the proposition which concerns man's actual obedience to one particular precept of the law, wherein will appear the third imperfection of man's obedience in fulfilling the moral law. We have seen that no man has perfect inherent sanctity free from nature's corruption. Again, no man can perform perfect actual obedience to all and every duty of the law without failing in any one point. And this much our adversaries will not hesitate much to yield unto us, confessing that there is no man but sins at some time or another, and that it is scarcely possible to avoid venial sins, as they call them. But then they deny utterly that a man sins in every particular good work. Though he cannot do all things perfectly, yet in some he may exactly fulfill the righteousness of the law, not missing in any one circumstance. And therefore, at least by that obedience, he may be justified.

This opinion of theirs neither has truth in itself, nor yet brings any benefit at all to their main purpose in proving justification by works. For to what end does it serve them to stand quarreling for the perfection of our obedience in one or two good works when yet we fail in many other things? One thing well done will not justify him who does many ill things. For that verse of James must be a truth: "He that keeps the whole law, and yet fails in one point, is guilty of all" (James 2:10). Much more guilty is he who keeps it in a few points, and breaks it in many. But yet further, we reject this opinion also as an error, and we teach the contrary: No man in this life can perform any one particular good work so exactly that in every point it shall answer the rigor of the law and the severe trial of God's judgment.

About this assertion our adversaries raise much stir and many foul slanders against us, proclaiming us to all the world as open enemies to all good works, that we are friends of the kingdom of darkness, promoting as much as in us lies all licentiousness in evil courses, and taking away the courage and endeavoring of men after pious duties. For who will set himself, they say, to do any good work if the Protestant's doctrine is true that in doing it he shall commit a mortal sin? Who will pray, fast, and give alms if when he does these things he cannot but sin? As good, then, it would be to do evil as to do good. A man can only sin, and so he shall do, regardless of whether he tries.

These slanderous incongruities fastened on us spring not out of our doctrine rightly understood, but out of froward and perverse hearts that will not see the truth. Such aspersions will easily be wiped off when, after the confirmation of the truth, we shall make answers to such objections as seem to infringe upon it. We say then that no man can perform any good work required in the law with such exact observation of every circumstance that (were it examined by the rigor of the law and God's justice) no fault at all can be found in it. This we prove by conscience, by Scriptures, and by reason.

First, we here appeal unto the conscience of man, the

judgment whereof is to be regarded, and whereunto we dare to stand in this matter. You who boast about such and such good works, that you have not committed any sin at all, do you indeed dare stand on it and upon these terms appear before God's judgment? Do you dare abide the strictness of this examination, standing ready to justify yourself against everything that He can object? Will you venture yourself upon this trial, even in the best works you do, that God cannot with His most piercing eye of justice spy a fault in them, and that if He numbers them He shall find nothing short? If He weighs them, do you believe He will not find one grain too light?

Again, let conscience speak. When you have prayed, fasted, given alms, or done any other excellent work of piety and charity in the most devout and blameless manner you think possible, do you think verily that in this case you do not stand in need of God's favor, and that you do not need to pray on your behalf, "Lord forgive me my trespasses"? What man would dare say or think, in any good work, "Lord, in this particular I do not desire that you should be merciful unto me"? Without doubt there is no man living upon earth who shall, in serious consideration of the severity of God's judgment and the great infirmity of his own nature, compare his own obedience with the severity of God's justice, but his heart will presently shrink within him and his conscience shun this trial as much as ever Adam did God's presence.

The thought of such a strict proceeding in judgment would make the proudest heart stop and tremble and the boldest face gather blackness, filling the soul with a horrible fear in the expectation of that day, should the most innocent life and the most holy actions of men be there scanned according to the rigor of justice, rather than graciously pitied, pardoned, and accepted, according to that merciful love of God which covers and passes by multitudes of sins. It would be arrogant pride in any man to utter that speech in a sober temper. Consider how Job breaks out in a passion, chafed by the sense of his miserable tortures and the froward disputes of his friends. "Oh," he says, "that a man might plead with God, as a man pleads with his neighbor" (Job 16:21). And, again, "Lay down now, put me in a surety with thee; who is He that will strike hands with me?" (Job 17:3). And, again, "Oh that I knew where I might find Him, that I might come even to His face! I would order my cause before Him and fill my mouth with arguments. I would know the words which He would answer me, and understand what He would say unto me" (Job 23:3–5).

Does the man speak reason or is he beside himself? What! Challenge God to dispute with him, and hope to make his party good in the quarrel? This was Job's infirmity. It is our adversaries' arrogance who dare set their foot against God's, and bid Him pry as narrowly as He will into their good works. They will maintain the righteousness thereof against all that He can object to prove the least sinfulness. Job saw his folly. God grant that these may see theirs.

In a calmer temper, when conscience was not overclouded with grief and anger, Job reads us a quite contrary lesson. "How should man be just with God? If He contend with him, he cannot answer Him one of a thousand" (Job 9:2–3). And, again, having reasoned and questioned God's wisdom and power, who is not to be questioned or resisted by any, he concluded, "How much less shall I answer Him, and choose out my words to reason with Him? Whom, though I were righteous, yet would I not answer, but I would make supplication to my Judge" (Job 9:14–15). Further, "If I would justify myself, mine own mouth will condemn me. If I say I am perfect, it shall prove me perverse. Though I were perfect, yet would I not know my soul; I would despise my life" (Job 9:20–21). And once more, "If I wash myself with snow water, and make my hands never so clean, yet shalt Thou plunge me in the ditch, and mine own clothes shall abhor me. For He is not a man as I am that I should answer Him, and we should come together in judgment" (Job 9:30–32).

See this holy saint, who elsewhere stands peremptorily in the defense of his innocence and uprightness against that wrongful imputation of hypocrisy which his friends charged him with, telling them that till he dies he will not take away his innocence from himself, nor shall his heart reprove him of his days. Yet when he sets himself before the tribunal of God's justice, he dares not stand out in his own justification, but submits himself to the mercy of his Judge with humble supplication for His favor. These confessions of Job are not compliments out of a feigned and needless modesty, but the fruits of a conscience rightly informed and apprehensive of its own sinfulness, and of the severe rigor of God's judgment.

The serious meditation on these two particulars we commend unto our adversaries, and all others of their humor who are apt to entertain favorable and gentle opinions concerning their sins, and withal to nourish high conceits of their own goodness. Whence they grow by degrees to think that God's judgment is like their own foolish imaginations; and where they, out of blindness or self-love, cannot see a fault, they presume that God Himself can find none. We hardly see beams in our own eyes; are we then so skillful as to spy the smallest mote? "Who can understand his faults?" said David (Psalm 19:2). Will you answer him, "I do!"? A secret fault may soon slip out; a deceitful heart may in one circumstance go beyond your wit and watchfulness. Here then humility would do well, and prayer for your ignorance and for your secret sins that are unknown to you as much as to others. Here true modesty would have her place, that you prefer God's wisdom and judgment above your own, remembering that He judges not as man judges, but somewhat other than you do, accounting that to be an abomination which in your own eyes is much prized. He always judges more exactly than you can, seeing much evil where you see little, and some evil where you think there is none. And therefore always speak to yourself in those excellent words of St. John: "If my heart condemn (as in many things it does), God is greater than my heart and knows all things" (1 John 3:20). God forbid, then, that in anything I should presume to plead with Him in my justification. "He is wise in heart and mighty in strength; who has hardened himself against Him and has prospered?" (Job 9:14). So much for our first argument, from the inward witness of the conscience, which in the most innocent life, often in the most holy work, draws back from God's judgment seat and is afraid to put itself upon the trial of His severe justice.

We have the Scriptures to witness unto us the same truth. "Hear my prayer, O Lord, give ear unto my supplication; in Thy faithfulness answer me and in Thy righteousness" (Psalm 143:1). Here the psalmist seems to appeal to the justice of God, requiring His help upon certain terms, as if God out of pure justice could not have denied him. But it is not so. It is the mercy of God that the holy prophet seeks. "Answer me in Thy faithfulness and righteousness," that is, "in those gracious promises wherein

No Man Can Perform a Good Work Perfectly

Thou hast made me to trust, whereupon I rely. Thou art just and faithful in keeping promises; be so to me in my distress, who according to Thy promise seek unto Thee for succor."

Unto this righteousness of God David presents himself and his supplication; but before that strict and severe justice of God he dares not stand, but in all submissiveness prays in the next words, "And enter not into judgment with Thy servant" (Psalm 143:2). He craves a merciful audience for his prayers, but deprecates the strict examination of his life and doings. He knows well that if God should deal with him upon so hard terms, his own innocence could never have made his prayers acceptable. "For," he says, "in this shall no man living be justified" (Psalm 143:2). The force of this passage Bellarmine seeks to evade by three poor, miserable shifts.

1. *David would not have God enter into judgment with him to judge him according to such things as he had of himself, but according to such things as God had given him.* That is, "Judge me not according to that righteousness which I have by nature, but according to that righteousness which Thou hast given by Thy grace." How ridiculous a fantasy this interpretation is, and quite beside the meaning of the prophet, it is easy for anyone to judge by reading that Psalm. Bellarmine, therefore, has another string to his bow, but it is as rotten as the former.

2. *The passage refers to venial sins which no man can avoid; though they are small faults, yet it is no injustice if God punishes them.* So the meaning is: "Lord, enter not into judgment," that is, "Lord, I will not contend with Thee. I confess myself to be a sinner and crave pardon. Divers small faults I have committed—not against the law, but aside from the law, and Thou mayest easily pardon them. My case is not

singular. I do therein but as other men do, among whom there is none so just but sometimes fails and offends. And therefore do not lay such faults to my charge."

Men of corrupt conscience thus sport with sin and play with the Scriptures. The Jesuit must bring us better proof than he does, else we shall never believe that David was a man of Bellarmine's mind concerning venial sins. That doctrine is part of the dregs of corrupted nature, maintained by Popish Moabites who are settled on their lies, infatuated by the love of sin, and flattering themselves in considering that wickedness to be little and light which God accounted as worthy to be hated. We acknowledge no venial sins but such as deserve eternal death, which hereafter we shall make good. And therefore, if David does not wish that God should enter into judgment with him because of venial sins that accompany his holiest practices, it is in effect that which we say; the difference is only in an epithet. We say David prayed not to come into judgment because his best works were sinful, and Bellarmine adds that they are venially or pardonably sinful. This helps him not a jot. For let him mince it how he desires, it is manifest that these were such sins as to cause David not to dare venture his best works to come unto the bar of God's severe judgment. But Bellarmine has yet another device.

3. *David speaks by comparison, that is, that though the righteousness of his works were true, being absolutely considered, yet being compared with God's righteousness it seemed to be unrighteousness* (as a candle set in the sun seems to have no light, and a little light compared to a greater one seems to be darkness).

We answer that David here makes a confession of his own sinfulness, not a comparison of his own righteousness with the righteousness of God. He desires that God will

No Man Can Perform a Good Work Perfectly

not enter into judgment with him not because he had less righteousness than God, in comparison to whom it seemed little or nothing, but because he was sinful and had not so much righteousness as he should. Many may have a righteousness of their own, infinite degrees below the righteousness of God, which yet may pass the trial of God's judgment without all reproof. This is manifest in the righteousness of Adam and in Christ's humanity, as both persons, though inferior to God's righteousness, were yet able to endure that strict examination. Wherefore we are not accounted as unjust for our imperfection because we have less righteousness than our Maker, but because we have not so much as we ought to have according to the capacity of our nature wherein He made us. But of this more hereafter. Let this serve as having clarified this first place of Scripture, and the objections against it.

The second passage of Scripture is: "But we are all as an unclean thing, and all our righteousness is as filthy rags; and we all do fade as a leaf, and our iniquities, like the wind, have taken us away" (Isaiah 64:6). This is the confession of the Church of God, submitting herself to Him in the acknowledgment of her sins and the justice of His anger against her. The confession is in every way general, both as for persons, with not one excluded ("we all are as an unclean thing") and likewise as for works, as none are excused from faultiness ("all our righteousness," nay, in the plural, "all our righteousnesses are as filthy rags"). Hence they acknowledge that God is justly angry with them, and that in His righteous displeasure they are afflicted, consumed, and brought into great adversity, the glory of the Church and state decaying more and more, like a fading leaf that falls from the tree and is driven away with the wind.

Against this plain acknowledgment of man's sinfulness in all his most righteous works the Jesuits take exception in various ways:

1. The prophet, they say, speaks here in the person not of the godly, but of the wicked, who make here this confession of their sin. And how do they prove this? Thus: the text says, "Behold, Thou art wroth, for we have sinned." Now God is not angry with the godly, but with the wicked. Again the text says, "There is none that calls upon Thy name," that is, none of the wicked persons, for the godly *do* call on God's name. But this exception is manifestly refuted by the whole order of the text, whereby it is apparent to any who have but half an eye that this recognition of sin and prayer for mercy are made by the whole church. All the faithful therein confess their own faults, as well as others, and sue for relief not only in behalf of others, but of themselves too (Isaiah 63:15–64:12). His reasons are worth nothing.

"God is not angry with the godly," says Bellarmine. No? Then Peter is in error who says, "The time is come that judgment must begin at the house of God; and if it begin at us, what shall the end of them be that obey not the gospel of God? And if the righteous be scarcely saved, where shall the ungodly and sinners appear?" (1 Peter 4:17–18). Here is judgment on God's house, that is, on the righteous who obey the gospel as well as on the ungodly who obey it not. And so it is that when the godly sin they smart for it in private afflictions and in public calamities; in both ways they find that God is not well pleased with their ill doings. When a church and a state are ruined, may not the most righteous take up this confession: "Lord, Thou art angry, for we have sinned. Even we by our sins have hastened and increased the public miseries"? I trust that none will deny it.

Again, the text speaks of those who do not call upon God's name. But the godly call upon it. Ergo, our opponents argue, it is not meant of them. True, they do call upon God's name; but is this done always with that diligence, with that zeal which God requires? How comes it to pass, then, that the godless men are many times secure, slothful, cold, and careless in the duties of God's most holy worship? Yea, in the corrupt and declining times of the church this problem is their fault chiefly who themselves begin to freeze in so general a coldness of the season, losing much of that fervency of Spirit which the apostle requires of us as at all times—especially when it should revive and put heat into others, when their love of religion begins to wax cold. At such times zeal in God's service—vehemence in prayer, constancy in all religious exercises, resolute but discreet forwardness in the holy profession of religion—is most commendable. But yet it so comes to pass that even then much security and slackness overcome the godly, and, while they should be a means to prevent a mischief, they hasten it upon themselves and others.

And thus the Jewish church here in this place confessed that there were none who called on the name of the Lord; a careless negligence and slackness in the service of God had come upon them, so that it is stated: "There were none that stirred up himself to take hold of God" (Isaiah 64:7). None awakened and roused himself with diligent endeavor to apply himself to the worship of God, a fault with which God may justly be angry as He then was. This first exception then is frivolous. The others that follow are just as idle.

2. By "all" in this place, they object, is to be meant the

greatest part; not all the Jews, nor all their works were sinful, but the greatest part. For so the word "all" is taken in some passages of Scripture, and therefore the Jesuits think it must needs be taken so here.

3. If it is meant of "all" simply, yet it is not to be understood at all times. All the people and their works were naught and sinful when they were to be carried away captive, but it does not follow that they were so at other times.

4. This reference must be restrained to the righteousness which consists in obedience to the ceremonial law. All our righteousness, that is, all our ceremonial works in sacrifices, observations of sabbaths, new moon, fasts, and so on are as filthy clothes, being done in that manner as we do them, without faith and obedience.

To these arguments we say that there would never be an end were a man bound punctually to refute every cavil which an adversary may frame out of his fanciful imagination and froward heart. We owe the Romanists no such credit as to assent to any point of religion upon their bare affirmation. We can as confidently deny such objections as these, without yielding them a refutation, as they do boldly make them without bringing any proof. And certainly most vain and ungodly is that course which our adversaries or any who tread in their steps do hold in their disputations about serious points of Christian doctrine. Being urged with convincing Scriptures, they think they have done the part of scholars, and satisfied the consciences of others desirous of truth, if they can amaze and astonish you a little with two or three interpretations and pretty exceptions, and so leave you to choose whichever interpretation you wish. They will not tell you which they will hold to, but even when their answers cross one another, yet they maintain that if one helps not, another

No Man Can Perform a Good Work Perfectly

may, and so they may altogether vex you when they cannot satisfy you. This quarrelsome humor of men who seek not the truth in love, but write to maintain disputes, is not the least vexation of the Spirit, and is weariness to the flesh of man, as all those will witness whose considerable reading has led them along into the perplexed mazes of school learning, whether divine or human.

The third passage of Scripture is, "If Thou, Lord, shouldst mark iniquities, O Lord, who shall stand?" (Psalm 130:3). This place is parallel to the previous one, wherein the holy prophet desires God to be attentive to the voice of his supplications and craves this audience merely of God's favor, not upon any righteousness or worth of his own. As for his merit, he confesses that if God should be strict to observe wherein he and all men go amiss, neither he nor anyone else would be able to stand in His presence. Hence he flies from God's justice to His mercy: "But there is forgiveness with Thee, that Thou mayest be feared" (Psalm 130:4). It is presumption then, and arrogant pride, for any Romanist to say, "Lord, if Thou observest iniquities, yet I shall be able to stand; in such and such good works be thorough in marking what is done amiss. I fear not the trial, nor will I sue for Thy mercy."

From Scripture arguments we come to reason this way: Wheresoever there is concupiscence and inordinate motions of the heart, wheresoever there is a defect of charity towards God and man, wheresoever venial sins (as our adversaries call them) are mingled with good works, there the best works of men are not free from some corruptions and sinfulness.

But in a regenerate man concupiscence and evil motions of the heart are present with him when he would do good. There is a want of that measure of love toward God and charity toward man which he might and ought to have. There also are, besides, many venial faults that accompany his best works. Ergo, the works of a regenerate man are not in every way good, but are in part sinful.

The minor premise is clear and confessed by our adversaries, especially with regard to concupiscence and imperfection of charity. As for venial sins, they also acknowledge it to be a very hard matter to avoid these in any good work. Wherefore they are driven in a desperate manner to deny the major premise and to avow that neither concupiscence nor imperfection of charity to God or our neighbor, nor yet venial sins mingled with good works, do at all impair the goodness and perfect righteousness of our obedience to the law, but that they are as good with those infirmities as without them. Bad causes must be helped out by bold and desperate attempts; and so it fares with our adversaries in this point. They will utterly deny that there is anything evil in a regenerate man rather than be forced to confess that there is anything evil in the works that he performs.

The impudent unreasonableness of their assertion we shall speak of shortly. In the meantime we go on unto the consideration of such arguments which are brought by our adversaries to prove that the good works of regenerate men are truly and perfectly good without all faultiness in them.

1. They prove it, then, first, from the examples of Job and David. Of Job it is said, "In all this Job sinned not, nor charged God foolishly" (Job 1:22). And, "In all this did not Job sin with his lips" (Job 2:10). As for David, he is conscious to himself of his own innocence and that no fault can be found in his doings, wherefore he prays, "Judge me, O Lord, according to my righteousness, and

No Man Can Perform a Good Work Perfectly

according to mine integrity that is in me" (Psalm 7:8). And after all this, he professes openly his innocence and reward for it. "I was," he says, "also upright before Him, and I kept myself from mine iniquity. Therefore has the Lord recompensed me according to my righteousness, according to the cleanness of my hands in His sight" (Psalm 18:23–24). And he declares how God had thoroughly tried him and yet found him faultless: "Thou hast proved mine heart; Thou hast visited me in the night; Thou hast tried me, and yet shall find nothing. I am purposed that my mouth shall not transgress" (Psalm 17:3).

How then can any man say that Job and David sinned mortally in their saying and doing when God Himself witnesses for them that they do not sin?

Hereto we answer that we do not lay sin unto the charge of those holy men, nor do we say they did ill, where the Scriptures witness they did well. Job, in that first act of his trial, acquitted himself well and overcame the temptation. He sinned not as afterwards he did, breaking forth into impatience; and that is all the Scripture meant by the words, "In all this Job sinned not." But whether Job's patience in this first conflict was in every way so unreprovable that not the least fault could be spied in it in God's severe judgment is more than we dare affirm, or our adversaries will ever be able to prove.

David's innocence in the time of Saul's reign was such that no imputation of unfaithfulness or ambition could justly be laid to his charge. Wherefore, when Saul's followers accused him of treason against their master, David appealed unto God, desiring Him to deal with him according to his innocence in that regard. His own conscience, and God with his conscience, after trial was made, acquitted him from plotting and practicing against Saul, as his adversaries said he did. Thence it follows that David did not offend in that way whereof his adversaries accused him. His heart was upright; his life was innocent; neither his adversaries could make proof, neither did his conscience accuse him or God condemn him of these faults that he was charged with. Thus far David dared to face God's judgment—that he was innocent in those particular evils whereof man had accused him. But it follows not, therefore, that he dared enter into judgment with God and plead that God Himself could find no fault at all with him. He might have many secret faults and imperfections, even in this most innocent passage of his life, which neither he nor his enemies could come to know; and therefore, though he dares to plead his righteousness before God, so far as man can accuse him of unrighteousness, yet he dares not go further to clear himself against all that God may object against him.

Hear what he himself says in this case: "Search me, O God, and know my heart; try me and know my thoughts" (Psalm 139:23). Does the prophet speak this out of confidence that God, upon search and trial, shall find no evil in his heart and thoughts? No, but out of holy desire that whatever evil is found in him may be amended. He knows well that many things may be found faulty in him, and therefore he stands not to justify himself, but only sues for grace to redress them, adding in the next words, "And see if there be any wicked way in me, and lead me in the way everlasting" (Psalm 139:24).

2. They prove that the works of regenerate men are not sinful by the Scriptures which call them "good works," and say that they are pleasing to God.

First, that they are good: "Let your light so shine before men, that they may see your good works" (Matthew

5:16). "Charge the rich that they do good, and be rich in good works" (1 Timothy 6:18). "We are His workmanship, created in Christ unto good works" (Ephesians 2:10). "Why trouble ye the woman? For she has wrought a good work upon me" (Matthew 26:10).

Second, that they are pleasing unto God is apparent by these verses: "Ye are made a holy priesthood to offer up spiritual sacrifices acceptable to God by Jesus Christ" (1 Peter 2:5). The apostle calls their alms sent to him "an odor of a sweet smell, a sacrifice acceptable, well-pleasing unto God" (Philippians 4:18). "To do good and to communicate forget not, for with such sacrifices God is well pleased" (Hebrews 13:16). Hence they argue that if the works of regenerate men are good and acceptable unto God, then certainly the Protestants err in their doctrine when they teach that the best works of men are sinful, since sin is neither good in itself nor in any way pleasing unto God, who is infinitely offended at all iniquities.

Hereunto we answer that this argument is nothing but a froward and willful misinterpretation of our doctrine. We teach that the best works of the best men are in part sinful. They thereupon cry out that we take away all goodness from the works of the godly, and that we account them to be damnable and mortal sins. This is a foolish calumny of men who cannot distinguish between the disease and the diseased body, but straightway conclude that the whole body itself is nothing else but a mere rotten ulcer because it has swellings and sores in some part of it.

Therefore, to unfold their eyes in this point, they are to understand that we make a necessary and true distinction between that which is sin and that which is sinful, teaching that the good works of the regenerate are not sins, though they are sinful. We explain it thus: It is to be called sin in its own nature, which is the transgression of the law in doing any act forbidden, or in leaving undone any act commanded by the law. The omitting or committing of any such act is properly a sin because it is directly and totally, in the very substance of it, against the law. Bellarmine falsely adds that God completely condemns deeds of alms done with a bad intention for vain glory. God does not condemn the work, but them for their ill doing of it.

As for praying to a false God, or neglecting prayer to the true God, both of them are sins in their very nature because both are forbidden by the moral law. We may call a work "sinful" if, even though its main substance is conformable to the law, it fails and offends against the law in some particulars related to the work. The thing may be done which the law commands, but not perfectly in every point as the law commands. Such a work, we say, is not a sin, though it is sinful. There is sin in it, but it is not all sin.

This distinction our adversaries cannot but admit as being in the works of the heathen and unregenerate Christians, and so in the good works of the regenerate themselves. We and they confess that the moral virtues of the heathen were good and commendable in the substance thereof, nor do we think there is any man so devoid of reason as to affirm that the justice, temperance, charity, and liberality of a heathen are mere vices and sins. We all grant that they were in every way virtues, but yet our adversaries themselves cannot affirm that they were in every way virtuous, free from all spots and stains of vice, since they had neither faith and sanctity from whence they sprang, nor the glory of God at which they aimed.

Now as the virtues of the natural man are in part

No Man Can Perform a Good Work Perfectly

stained with vice, so the good works of the regenerate man are in part sinful. To fast, to pray, and to give alms, along with the like works of piety and mercy, we affirm and teach are good works—good in their nature and use, being such actions as the law commands. We know none of our side to be so far gone with passion as to maintain that a godly man sins because he fasts, prays, and gives alms, as if those very acts were nothing but damnable sins. We detest such frantic opinions, and if any of our writers have let slip such words as may give occasion to our adversaries so to think of us, we do not, nor are we bound to, justify every hot and choleric speech breathed out in eagerness of disputation. Good works they are, truly and verily good, but they are not perfectly good.

When a good man prays he does well, but he never does so well that he may not do better. Nor dares any man in the world avow either that the root whence good actions come is purged by perfect holiness, or that the manner of doing them is so exactly kept in a precise observation of every circumstance, or the end in doing them (God's glory and man's good) so sincerely and truly aimed at that the severity of God's justice cannot find the least failing in any of those things. This is all we teach regarding the sinfulness of good works, and this we hold to as a most certain truth. And we say that this sinfulness accompanying our good works is sufficient to bar us from justification by them. For we deserve no reward for what is well done unless all was well done. But nevertheless it shall not hinder God's gracious acceptance of our good works, who is well-pleased with the obedience of His children so far as it is good and holy; and when it fails, for Christ's sake He mercifully pardons their trespasses. So much for the second argument.

3. The third is from reason grounded on Scripture. Where there are sufficient causes and means of well-doing, they argue, there a good work may be done without all fault. But in a regenerate man there are causes and means sufficient for well-doing. Ergo, he may do well and not offend.

They prove the minor premise as follows: For the performance of any good work, there is required nothing but these things: knowledge of what is to be done, will and power to do it. But now a regenerate man has all these. For, first, his understanding is enlightened so that he can easily know what is good to do. Second, his will and affections are sanctified and aided by grace to desire and endeavor the performance of it. And, third, and last, he has power to put in practice what he knows and desires, there being no impediment, inward or outward, that should hinder him. Ergo, he may do well and sin not.

Here we desire that they show us how a regenerate man is endued with such perfect abilities as may help him and quite rid him of all such impediments as might hinder him in well-doing.

This, they say, is done by the grace of sanctification given unto a regenerate man whereby he is freed from all contagion of sin and such encumbrances as hinder him in well-doing. For by this grace given to him he is made a good tree. Now "a good tree cannot bring forth bad fruit" (Matthew 7:18), and therefore a good man cannot do bad works. Again, he is made a fruitful branch of Christ, the true Vine. As it is said, "I am the Vine, ye are the branches. He that abides in Me, and I in him, the same bears much fruit" (John 15:5). And, therefore, that fruit is only good, and the similitude of a branch much illustrates the matter (in their imagination). For with as a vine branch, if first it

No Man Can Perform a Good Work Perfectly

has sufficient moisture from the body of the vine, if (second) it has sufficient heat from the sun to digest that moisture, and, third, if it is not hurt nor hindered by frosts, wet, winds, worms, or other such discommodities of the air and soil—then certainly it will bear very much and very good fruit.

So it is in a regenerate man, they say. From Christ he receives sufficient moisture of divine grace which is in him, as a well of water "springing up unto everlasting life" (John 4:14). He has sufficient heat of spiritual affection to cause him to bud forth into good works. For Christ says, "I am come to send fire on earth, and what will I if it be already kindled?" (Luke 12:49). And "Did not our hearts burn within us?" said the two disciples who went to Emmaus (Luke 24:32). Therefore they have heat enough. Finally, they have no impediments. Not inward, for "There is no condemnation to them that are in Christ Jesus" (Romans 8:1). Not outward, for it is written, "Nothing shall separate us from the love of God that is in Christ Jesus our Lord" (Romans 8:38). Therefore, there is no inward or outward impediment to good works.

Hereunto we make answer that this argument is a sophistic cavillation, which proves that which we do not deny. They say that a regenerate man has sufficient principles of right and honorable working. We say so too, confessing that he is made a good tree and a fruitful branch, that he is enlightened, sanctified, and strengthened by the Spirit of God unto the performance of good works. We grant that now he is enabled to do well who, before his regeneration, could do nothing but ill. But the question still remains whether now he does so well that he does nothing ill when he does best. We grant that the vine which in former time yielded nothing but wild grapes, now being transplanted and grafted into the best Vine, bears good grapes. But we deny that they are so sweet and kindly in every respect as not to have a little relish still of their former wildness and sourness.

Wherefore our adversaries do but trifle with us to tell us that a regenerate man has sufficient means to do good works. This we deny not; but we question whether they have sufficient help to perform any work so absolutely and perfectly good that God Himself cannot charge it with any sin at all. This we constantly deny. And as for their discourse that a regenerate man has sufficient knowledge, power, and will to do good perfectly, in this they affirm more than will ever be proved. Our imperfections in every one of these three particulars, witnessed to our conscience by Scripture and experience, disable us ever from doing any entirely and totally good work. Knowledge we have, but much darkened by ignorance. We have a will to do good, but that also is corrupted with much froward rebellion. We have a power to do good, but it is always crossed and much restrained by manifold lusts within and temptations without. How is it possible for us, being compassed about with so many infirmities, not to offend in one thing or another.

Becanus here gives us an instance of a good work and bids us show what sin there is in it. If, he says, a regenerate man reads or hears the words of Christ (in Matthew 6) to give alms, he, being enlightened, knows that this is a worthy and honest work. Whereupon he is touched in heart and stirred up to do it. He consents to this motion and resolves upon the execution, which (supposing that he is rich) nothing can now hinder, because he is both able and willing to give.

Now, then, these alms being thus given out of knowl-

No Man Can Perform a Good Work Perfectly

edge, and from a pious motion of the heart tending to God's honor and our neighbor's good, the Jesuit desires to know of us where there is any sin it. We say there is some evil in every good work, and therefore he would have us tell him what evil there is in this alms-deed. Unto this we say that this inquiry of the Jesuit is the most ridiculous and absurd thing that can be. He asks us where the sin is. What if we answer him, "We do not know"? Is he now ever the wiser? What has he gained thereby? Are other men's works without all faults because we know not what the faults are? No. Are they without fault because they know not whether there are any within them or not? What silliness would it be to argue in this way!

Therefore, when we come to this point of strictly examining the works of men, first, we tell the Jesuit that he must not put forth hypothetical cases (suppose that such a good work be done so and so, what then?). We dispute now concerning particulars in every man's real practice. The inquiry is not in general (what evil is there in such and such a good work, done thus and thus, according as the circumstances are framed in an imagined case). To ask what sin is there in an alms-deed done out of faith and charity to God's glory—this is a fond question when thus framed upon general terms. We can say there is no sin in it. But the inquiry is in particular: What evil is there in such a work done by this or that man, according to all circumstances that were at that time incident to the work? For example, what sin was there in Zacchaeus' or Cornelius' alms-deeds? This question we admit and answer to it that there was some sin for which those holy men, as well as others, would not have been willing that God should enter into judgment with them, strictly to judge them.

"Yes, but," the Jesuits will reply, "name what sin this was or else you wrong them."

Now this is mere impudence. For who is judge of the actions? Are we? Or are God and their own consciences? We can be no judges who at best can judge according to outward appearances. We know not their hearts, nor are we privy unto every particular circumstance that accompanied those actions of theirs. Circumstances in every particular action differ infinitely. One man may offend in this point, another in that. Nor have we a general rule whereby to judge alike of all. And therefore it is a childish query to ask one man whether another man offends who may do evil a thousand times, not only secretly from others, but while unaware of it himself.

If then the Jesuit will have an answer to his question, he must resort to particular men's consciences and to God. For only the spirit of man and the Spirit of God know the things of man. Let him ask a Cornelius when he gives alms whether he thinks this work is so well done that no fault can be found with it. Doubtless he will answer that he cannot excuse himself from all faultiness; though he knew no specific charge against himself, yet he dares not stand to God's judgment. His confession and prayer would in this case be the same as that of Nehemiah: "Remember me, O my God, concerning this also, and spare me according to the greatness of Thy mercy" (Nehemiah 13:22). He at once begs favorable acceptance of his obedience and gracious pardon of his infirmities. If this does not sufficiently conclude the argument, let the Jesuit repair to God Almighty and ask Him, "Where is the sin in such and such a good work?" God no doubt can shape him an answer that will soon confound his pride and folly, and make it quickly appear unto him that sinful

No Man Can Perform a Good Work Perfectly

man, when he pleads with God, is not able to answer him one objection of a hundred that God shall make against him. This answers the third argument, that man has sufficient means to do well and not sin.

4. The last argument is drawn from such absurdities as they say follow upon our doctrine. Thus, if (they say) our doctrine is true that the best works of men are sinful, then these absurdities are likewise true doctrine: that to be justified by faith is to be justified by sin; that no man ought to believe because the work of believing is sin; that all good works are forbidden because all sin is forbidden; that God should command us to commit sin because He commands us to do good works; that God, in bidding us to be zealous of good works, should in effect bid us to be zealous of mortal sin; that to pray for the pardon of sin is a damnable sin. These and other such absurd positions would be true if the Protestant's doctrine concerning the sinfulness of good works is granted.

Hereunto we answer that these absurdities issue not out of our doctrine, but out of our adversaries' malicious imaginations. They are like the raging sea, casting up mire and dirt from its own bottom, and would fain throw all this filth in the face of the Reformed churches to make them odious and hateful to the world. The best thing is that truth cannot be disgraced, though it can belied. These soul absurdities touch us not, but follow upon that doctrine which is none of ours, namely that the good works of the regenerate are in their very nature altogether sin and nothing else but uncleanness, filth, and unadulterated iniquities.

Such an absurd assertion would indeed yield such an absurd consequence. But we defend it not, and they abuse us grossly when in their writings they report of us the contrary to what we maintain. This only we teach, that men's good works are in part sinful. Much good they have in them, but withal some evil mingled therewith. Among the gold some dross also will be found that will not be able to abide the fire of God's severe trial. Imperfections will appear in our best works so long as human infirmity and mortality hang upon us. This we teach, and from this doctrine all who have reason may see that no such unreasonable conclusions can be collected.

And let this suffice to confirm this third proposition concerning the imperfection of our obedience to the moral law of God, even in the good works which we perform. From this truth every godly heart should learn both Christian humility and also industry: first, humility not to boast in the flesh and glory in its own righteousness, thinking that God highly accounts of, and rewards largely, that which is very little worth; second, industry in a faithful endeavor after perfection, so that what cannot be done as well as it ought may yet every day be done better than it was before.

Chapter 10

Three Objections to the Truth Answered

Thus we have discoursed at length in the confirmation of our second argument, concerning the impossibility of man's fulfilling the law in this life, and so consequently of justification by the law. Against all that has been said in proof of this point, our adversaries have three common and general objections:

1. Concupiscence, or natural corruption in the first and second act of it, is not sin.

2. Imperfection in our charity and obedience is not sin.

3. Smaller faults, or (as they call them) venial sins, do not hinder the justice and goodness of any good work.

To these three positions they have continual recourse. For whereas they cannot deny but that there is in the regenerate both a proneness of nature unto evil and also many inordinate sinful motions arising thence, they first deny that either of these natural corruptions or disordered motions of the heart are sin.

Again, they confess that no man has such perfect love of God and man but that he may increase in charity; nor are his good works so perfectly good but that they ought still to strive to do them better. But then here also they deny that this imperfection of our charity and good works is sin.

Lastly, they grant that no man can avoid venial sins, even in the best works he does. But then they deny that venial sins are contrary to the law, so that, even though a man commits them, yet he may perfectly fulfill the law of God.

I cannot go into great depth in refuting these foul errors. The confutation of them belongs properly to the article on remission of sins, where the nature and kinds of sins are to be handled. For the present I shall touch on them briefly and proceed to the matter.

1. As for the first point, we defend this conclusion: the vicious inclination and proneness of nature unto evil, as also the inordinate motions of concupiscence which goes before consent, are sins even in a regenerate man.

That the inclination and proneness of nature to sin is a sin we prove thus. First, it is expressly so called by the apostle not once or twice, but in almost every verse of Romans 7: "I am carnal, sold under sin"; "the sin that dwelleth in me"; "the law of sin" (Romans 7:14, 20, 23, 25). In itself it is sin, and deserves the wages of sin, eternal death. For this cause the apostle there calls it "the body of death" (Romans 7:24), because this inward corruption (which is like a body that has many members, consisting of diverse evil affections spreading themselves throughout his whole nature) made him liable unto eternal death, from which only God's mercy in Christ could deliver him.

Second, to rebel against the law is sin. Therefore to have a rebellious inclination is likewise sin. For if the act is evil, the habit must be also. If the law forbids one, it must forbid the other. If it is evil to break one commandment in act, is it not evil to have a proneness and readiness of mind to break it? The habit identifies a man as sinful, not the act. Nor does God abhor any less the proneness of man to offend Him than we abhor the ravenous disposition of a wolf, though it is a cub not yet used to the prey, or one tied up in a chain and kept from ravening.

Third, the evil motions of the heart without consent are sins since they are forbidden in the moral law, in the Tenth Commandment, "Thou shalt not covet." For motions with consent are forbidden in the other commandment, as appears manifestly in Christ's exposition of the commandments where not only the outward act of adultery, but the inward desire is also forbidden (Matthew 5:28), if we believe Christ, the best Interpreter of the law. When then the Tenth Commandment forbids coveting our neighbor's wife, it either means the same kind of lusting, with a needless tautology, or a different type, that which is not consented unto. Nor can our adversaries shift this off, though Becanus most impudently denies it without any reason.

Fourth, whatsoever is inordinate and repugnant to right reason is sin. But these motions without consent are inordinate; ergo they are sin.

The minor premise is confessed, that these motions are disordered and repugnant to right reason. The major premise is apparent. For what is order and right reason in morals or customs but that course of doing anything which is conformable to God's law and His will? God is the God of order. His law is the rule of order in all human actions. What is right reason but the conformity of man's understanding and will unto God's will, which alone is the rule of righteousness? We never purpose and will matters rightly but when we will them agreeably to God's will. Wherefore it is a gross absurdity to deny the sinfulness of these disorderly motions, seeing that no man can break those orders which God has made and yet be faultless. Nor is it possible that a man should do that which is contrary to God's will and yet be without sin in doing it. These motions, then, without consent are confusions in nature, opposite to the righteousness of the will of God and unto that even and straight order expressed in His law.

We conclude then that concupiscence and inordinate motions of the soul not consented unto are sins, contrary to our adversaries' assertion. They bring some reasons to prove that they are not.

ARGUMENT 1. Original sin is taken away in baptism, but concupiscence is not taken away in baptism, as appears by experience in the regenerate in whom it remains. Ergo, concupiscence and proneness to sin is no sin.

This argument is frivolous. In original sin there are two things—first, the guilt; second, the inherent corruptions. We say that in baptism the guilt is altogether washed away from the baptized elect by the blood of Christ. And so the corruption thereof is in part taken away by the sanctifying Spirit of Christ, poured out upon the regenerate, which by degrees purges out the inherent sinfulness of nature by replanting the graces of sanctification in all parts. Concupiscence, then, notwithstanding baptism, remains in the regenerate and is a sin in them, the guilt whereof God mercifully pardons in Christ.

ARGUMENT 2. What is not in our power to avoid, God does not forbid us by His law. But it is not in our power to avoid the motions of the heart that precede reason and consent. Ergo, they are not sins forbidden us.

To this we answer that the major premise is true in things merely natural, that fall out by the necessity of nature well-disposed. So, we say, God's law would be uncouth should He command a man never to be hungry or thirsty, which things he cannot avoid, but which come upon him by the mere necessity of nature. But concerning inordinate motions there is no such matter. God has laid

Three Objections to the Truth Answered

no such necessity on nature in her creation, but we, by our sins, have brought it upon ourselves.

Thus no such necessity excludes us. In this case it helps a man no more to say, "I cannot avoid evil thoughts and desires," than it does a desperate sinner who by continuance has hardened himself in evil courses, or than it helps the devils and the damned if they should say, "We cannot choose but to do evil."

ARGUMENT 3. That which would have been natural and without fault in man if he had been created without sin is not sin. But motions preceding consent would be natural and without fault in men so made. Ergo, in us they are not faults in themselves.

Here our adversaries have made a man of white paper, or like the first created matter, a man who has no quality in him morally good or bad, that is, a man who does not have the image of God in either knowledge, righteousness, or holiness engraved upon his understanding, will, affections, or whole person. Nor yet is there in him any contrary evil quality that comes upon him by reason of such a defect. Now regarding such a concoction they dispute. If God had created a man thus, neither good nor bad, what then? As the old saying goes, "If the heavens fall, we shall have larks quite cheap." Suppositions framed by our imaginations regarding what might be done are vain and needless when we see what is done.

This we see: Man was created in God's image, invested with all real qualities of righteousness and holiness. This we see also: Man, being fallen, is born in original corruption, deprived of God's image, and thereupon depraved in his whole nature by sinful infirmity. A man in his pure nature, one who has neither grace nor corruption, was never found in this world, Yea, it is a contradiction to imagine a man thus naked without his qualities: that he has reason, but neither enlightened nor darkened; a will, but merely indifferent, neither inclined to good or evil; affections, but neither virtuously nor viciously disposed. In a word, he is a man capable of virtue or vice, holiness or sinfulness, and yet has neither. That would be to make a man little better than an unreasonable beast.

But let us pursue the argument a little. Suppose that a man was made in his pure nature; would such disorderly motions be found in him? Yes, they say, and that boldly. If man were created by God in pure natural parts, without doubt God would have established man's spirits and flesh in two parts repugnant to each other (i.e., standing against, opposite to each other). And he would have two contrary appetites, the rational and the sensual or emotional; therefore he would naturally have certain motivations which are repugnant to reason. Without doubt, the Jesuit is deceived in his imagination, and his argument is not worth a button. A man in his pure nature would have two parts, a soul and a body, spirit and flesh. He would have two appetites, rational and sensual. Therefore, they say, these parts, in their motions and desires, would be contrary one to the other. But this consequence is false. They would be different, not opposite and repugnant to each other. The body and the senses would lead a man to those things that are agreeable to the body. The soul and rational appetite, or will, would incline him to those higher and more noble objects agreeable to the soul. But neither of these inclinations would cross and trouble one another. The inferior faculties, like the lower spheres, would move differently from the superior, but yet most orderly according to their own nature, without impeaching the motions of the other. Each faculty in its place would work in an orderly fashion, in sweet harmony and agreement each with the other, had not sin brought confusion and discord into the world. As it is between God and man, so it is between man and himself.

This we further make good by this argument. Whatsoever is natural, and so without blame in man, that Christ took upon Himself. But these inordinate motions of the sensual appetite, repugnant unto will and reason, Christ did not take upon Himself. Ergo, they are not natural and without blame.

The major premise of this syllogism we prove by this: "He was made like unto man" (Philippians 2:7); "In all things it behooved Him to be made like unto His brethren" (Hebrews 2:17); and "We have not a High Priest which cannot be touched with a feeling of our infirmities, but was in all things tempted in like sort, yet without sin" (Hebrews 4:15). Whence it is manifest that Christ, in taking upon Himself our nature, took upon Himself all the properties of our nature and, withal, such infirmities of our nature as are not sinful in themselves, or the effects or punishments of sin in us. If therefore it is natural in man that the motions of the sensual appetite should accompany and be repugnant unto reason, and that this is no sin unless consent makes it so, then certainly Christ had in Him such motions and inordinate desires. But to affirm that there were in Christ such disorderly motions of His inferior faculties, repugnant unto His reason and will, is a blasphemy against the immaculate Lamb of God. Christ was indeed tempted (as the text says) and in like sort as we are. But will any man here understand this of inward temptations arising from anything within Christ, as if He were, like us, drawn aside with concupiscence and enticed (James 1:14), the motions of His emotional faculties inclining Him to that which was contrary to His understanding and will? We confess that He was fiercely tempted by Satan and wicked men from without; but that He was tempted by anything in Himself, by disorderly motions of His heart tending unto evil and checked by His will and reason—this we account an abominable error concerning the spotless humanity of our Savior. We deny that in Him there ever was the least disorderly desire, thought, word, or work whatsoever. And therefore we conclude that such motions are not natural unto men, becoming sinful only by accident because they are consented unto; rather they are accidental unto men, being the fruit of original corruption, and are in themselves verily and properly sins.

ARGUMENT 4. To conclude this point, let us hear that argument which Bellarmine makes: "Where there is no law, there is no sin" (Romans 4:15). But there is no law prescribed unto sense and sensual appetites. Ergo, the motions thereof are not sinful.

The major premise we grant. The minor premise he proves by saying that the law presupposes reason in all that whereto it is given. But the sensual part of man is without reason, and therefore no more capable of obeying law than are brute beasts, to whom therefore no law is given. This he further proves from Romans 7:20: "Now if I do that I would not, it is no more I that do it, but sin that dwelleth in me." Here it is plain (says Bellarmine) that the apostle did not sin because he lusted against his will. It was not he who did the work, but it was the sin in him. Wherefore Paul says afterward that in his mind, i.e., in his superior faculties, he served the law of God and kept it, although in his flesh, i.e., his sensual appetite and inferior faculties, he served the law of sin. Yet, for all that, he sinned not in so doing because sin cannot be but in the mind, and the law is not given to those faculties that are without reason.

To this we answer that God gives no law to irrational creatures, but to such as have reason. The sensual faculties of brute beasts have no other rule than nature's instinct, which guides and moderates their several motions in due order and measure. But in man those inferior faculties, however irrational, are yet capable of reason's government which, according to God's law, prescribes unto the motions of the sensual appetite their measure and bounds, beyond which they may not pass. If a man were uncorrupted, the appetite would obey this rule of reason and keep itself within those prescribed bounds. But, being now corrupted by sin, it breaks out beyond this compass and overbears reason and will, which in their sinful weakness are not able to bridle these unruly motions. Wherefore, when Bellarmine says that the law is given to the rational will, not to the sensual appetite, it is utterly false, because in man it is capable of government and so subject to the law. Our reason has even in this corrupted state a civil command over our appetite and affections, so that it can moderate them by fair persuasions now and then. That which it can do sometimes, it ought to do always; and if any affections can obey reason at some times, if they were not infected with sin, they would do it at all times. And if they do well when they obey, certainly they do evil when they disobey. And therefore, such motions of them as are repugnant to right reason are nothing but rebellion against God's law.

As for the passage in Romans 7, we answer that the interpretation of it which Bellarmine brings is most perverse and against all sense. The apostle complains that he did the evil which he would not; no doubt in so doing he did sin. But what is it now which committed this guilt or sin? "It is not I who do it," says the apostle, "but that sin that dwells in me." That is, according to Bellarmine, not I in my mind or superior faculties of reason and will, but my inferior appetite and affections which do this evil against my consent. So the meaning shall be that by concupiscence in that duel the apostle committed sin, but the apostle himself committed it not, which is very absurd—as if a choleric man, having done a mischief in his anger, should say it was not he who did it, but his raging passion. Or this would be like an adulterer saying that it was not he who committed the sin, but his sinful affection that carried him further than reason would.

So, our adversaries claim, if God will punish such a sin, He must not punish the person, but only his sensual appetite which was at fault. That is ridiculous. Not only does it contradict the Romish doctrine manifestly in teaching that such disorderly motions of the sensual appetites are not sins (which the apostle here rejects, saying plainly that what dwelt in him and did the evil he would not, was still his sin), but it draws after it another gross error, namely, that some faculties in man may sin and yet the man not sin himself. The apostle, when he says that "it is not I who do it, but sin in me," does not oppose one faculty against the other, the rational will against the sensual appetite, seeking for a shift to excuse his sin by putting it off from himself to that which was not capable of sin. Rather he opposes grace in every faculty to corruption in the same faculty as two contrary principles and causes of his actions—one moving to good, the other inclining to bad.

Hence the apostle says that when he does evil, "it is not I who do it," i.e., "I, regenerate according to the grace that dwells in me, for that inclines me to do good. But it is the sin dwelling in me which, when I would do well, inclines me to do evil." He here shows the root from whence this evil comes, but yet he does not put off the fault from himself. As it is he who does well, so it is he who does ill too. Accordingly he concludes, "Then I myself do both well and ill. Well according to grace in my mind, that is, the regenerate part both of inferior and superior faculties serves the law of God; but ill according to corruption remaining in me, in my flesh, the unregenerate part, the law of sin" (see Romans 7:25). Much more might be added, but it is not my purpose here to extend this into a lengthy discussion.

2. I proceed to the second objection of our adversaries who teach that, although our love of God is imperfect, yet this imperfection is not sin in us. They grant that no man has any grace of the Spirit but he may increase in it daily; that the love of God and our neighbors may still grow on to further degrees of affection; that no grace or good work has that full perfection which it might have in this life, or which we shall attain unto in heaven. But they deny that this defect is any fault or sin.

The defect in love is that we do not do our works earnestly with as much choice or pleasure as we do our works which are for our own benefit—this is a defect indeed, but it is a fault and not a sin. Our love, even compared to the love of the blessed ones, is imperfect; nevertheless it can be said to be absolutely perfect.

This is an error against which we defend the following conclusion in general, concerning both charity and all man's righteousness: The defect or want of perfection in man's righteousness is sin. For the proof of this point we are to observe that the imperfection or perfection of anything is to be considered in two ways:

Comparatively, when anything compared to another is more or less perfect than that other.

Absolutely, when considered in itself it has or lacks that perfection which it should have by its proper nature.

Between these there is a great difference. For comparative imperfection is not evil; absolute imperfection is evil. We may see this in an example. When the senses that are in man are compared with their equivalents in other creatures, it is manifest that ours are much exceeded by them, as by an eagle for sight, a spider for touch. Here we say that the eye of a man is not so perfect as the eye of an eagle, but yet we do not account this imperfection to be any natural evil of the eye of a man. God might have given a stronger and a clearer sight to men, but we do not blame His works nor count our sight imperfect because it does not have that singular temper which is in other creatures, but because it lacks at any time that temper which is agreeable to our nature. Such a defect is properly an evil nature only when something is wanting, with regard to the perfection of any part, which by the course of nature should be there.

Thus it is also in grace. If we compare the righteousness of man or angels with the righteousness of God, we say that God is infinitely more perfect than the creatures. But now is this imperfection in human or angelic righteousness any evil and sin in them? We say no. Neither are the angels sinful because they are less righteous than God, nor is Adam sinful because he is less righteous than both. God made them both less good than Himself, yet very good and without all sin. There are degrees of righteousness, and though the creature is infinitely below the highest pitch of goodness (which is God), yet he may still be above that lowest descent unto sin and unrighteousness. In philosophy we dispute whether the slackening of any degree in one quality is the mingling of another that is contrary—for example, if heat of eight degrees is decreased to seven, whether there is any degree of cold mingled with it. It is hard to say that there is. But concerning grace and righteousness it is certain that there is remission of degrees without any mingling of sin and iniquity. As the holiness of saints is less than that of angels, that of angels is less than the holiness of Christ's glorified humanity, and this is less than His deity. And yet in the least of these righteousnesses there is no unrighteousness at all to be found, no, not even in the severe judgment of God, unless we say there is unrighteousness in heaven, where no unclean thing can enter.

Well, then, what imperfection of man's righteousness is it which is sin? We say there is imperfection when man, in any grace or good work, lacks that degree of goodness which he ought to have. In nature, if the eye lacks the clearness of sight which should be in it, it is a natural evil. In morality, if a man lacks that temperance or degree of temperance that he ought to have, it is a vicious and moral evil. So in grace, the lack of that righteousness or degree of righteousness which God requires to be in man is a sin and spiritual evil. All such privations of what should be present are evil in whatsoever kind. If they are in nature, they are things to be pitied in their evil; they deserve pity and cure. If in virtue and grace, they are things to be blamed in their evil and are worthy of blame and punishment. Such defects as these in grace, when man falls short not only of that which is in others, but that which should be in himself, always arise from the mixture of corruption and sin.

When someone does not love God or his neighbor as much as he ought to, it is because his heart is wicked, at least in part, and because he loves other things more than he should. These things are certain and undeniable, according to those words of St. Augustine, which are authentic: "It is a sin, either when it is not love, as it should be, or when it is less than it should be." It is a sin not to love God at all, or to love Him less than we should.

Wherefore here we ask the Jesuit whether charity and other graces in a regenerate man are as perfect in this life as they ought to be. If he says they are not as perfect as they ought to be, how can he affirm that this defect is no fault nor sin? Can a man possibly do worse or be worse than he should, and yet be in no fault as a result? If he says they are as perfect as they should be, his own conscience, and the consciences of all the men in the world, will gainsay him for a liar. No man can say that he loves God and his neighbor as much as he ought to, and that he is not bound in every grace and good work to arrive at greater perfection than he has at the present. He who thinks himself nearest unto the mark will yet be driven to confess that he falls many bows short of those patterns which he ought to imitate: Adam in his innocence, Christ's humanity, and the saints in heaven. We here bid them tell us the point where we shall stop, such that when we have come so far we need seek no further perfection. If they cannot do this, then they must confess, as the truth is, that every man is bound by God's command to be more holy, to be more perfect in all grace and good works. And so far as he lacks any degree or dram of goodness that should be in him and his works, so far he is sinful and guilty of a fault.

Three Objections to the Truth Answered

3. I go on to the last assertion of our adversaries, which concerns venial sins, that these do not hinder the righteousness of man's good works. A man may be a perfectly just man, they argue, though he commits many venial sins. Their reason is that venial sins are not contrary to charity, the love of God and our neighbor, and so may stand well enough with the fulfilling of the law.

Against this error, tending to the obduration of man's heart in impenitence and love of sin, we maintain this conclusion: Those sins which the Church of Rome calls venial truly make a regenerate man and his works unrighteous in the sight of God.

This we prove by this one argument: Whosoever transgresses the law is unrighteous in so doing. But he who commits venial sins transgresses the law. Ergo, he who commits venial sins is an unrighteous man.

The major premise is undeniable. As for the minor premise, our adversaries are in a quandry. They are loath to grant it, yet cannot tell how to deny it with any honesty. Bellarmine, after one or two shuffling distinctions, at last plainly denies that venial sins are contrary to the law. In answer to the words of James that "in many things we offend all," and to that statement of John that "if we say we have no sin, we deceive ourselves," he says that these passages are actually opposed to the view that venial sins are properly against the law. Such as are of that opinion, let them consider, he says, what they will answer to James 2:10: "He that keeps the whole law, and yet offends in one point, is guilty of all." Therefore the solid response is, he says, that venial sins, without which one does not live, are not straightforwardly sins, but imperfectly so, and, according to this manner, are not against the law, but beyond the law. And thus, he says, "They all stick together (like pebbles in a band), for he who offends in one area, truthfully transgressing one precept, is reckoned of it all, and straightforwardly he is established as unjust—and nonetheless we all offend in many things; indeed notwithstanding even if we do nothing contrary to the law, nevertheless we do many things beyond the law. And he who was born of God does not sin by transgressing the law, and nevertheless if we say we have no sin by doing nothing beyond the law (that is, even if we say we are sinless because we did not even sin beyond the law), we seduce ourselves and the truth is not in us."

This is an unbound broom, as will appear by undoing that distinction which seems to hold it together. Venial sins are not against the law, but besides the law, Bellarmine says. Well, we must now know what is against the law and what is besides it. That is against the law when anything is done which the law forbids or left undone which it commands. That is besides the law when the thing done is neither commanded nor forbidden in the law. He then who commits a venial sin does some such act as the law neither forbids nor commands. Here then we ask, "Are venial sins sins?" Yes. Is God offended with them? Yes, and He may justly punish them with the loss of heaven. For so Bellarmine himself confesses: "Venial sins, unless they are mercifully remitted, impede one from entering into His kingdom, into which nothing contaminated may enter." Now surely this is amazing—that such acts as these should defile a man, deserve hell, offend God, in a word be sins, and yet for all this be neither commanded nor forbidden in any law of God. Was ever such a toy heard of as this concept of "sins beyond the law"? It is a most ridiculous contradiction. He who does anything beside the law, not mentioned nor included

Three Objections to the Truth Answered

therein by way of prohibition or command, clearly does not sin nor offend at all. For whom does he offend, or who can accuse him of sin? Does God the Lawgiver? No, for it was not His intention to command or forbid such an act, and therefore, be it done or not done, it does not cross His will, nor has He any reason to find fault or be displeased at it.

Satan or man cannot accuse him, for let them then show the law that proves him to be an offender. If they cannot allege a law against which he has transgressed, they wrongfully accuse him of a fault. Would it not be an absurd accusation against a prisoner at the bar to say that he has indeed done nothing against the laws of the land, but that he has done many things besides the law, not forbidden nor commanded in the law, and deserves to be punished for it as an offender?

But now if those venial sins are mentioned in God's law, then such actions are either commanded or forbidden. If commanded, then not doing such a thing is plainly contrary to the law. For example, to steal a penny or some other small matter, to speak an idle word, to tell an officious lie—these are venial sins, say our adversaries. But how do they know they are sins? Who told them so? The Scriptures, they will say. Where? In the Eighth and Ninth Commandments. Ask them now, "Did God intend in those commandments to forbid those actions of stealing and lying, yes or no? If He intended it not, then it is not sin at all to do them, because it does not cross God's will or offend Him. If He did intend to forbid us those things, then to do them is a sin, manifestly contrary to the holy will of God, the Lawgiver."

Wherefore let us here remember that excellent rule of Bernard: "For things not commanded, we may either lawfully do them or leave them; but for things commanded, to neglect them is a sin; to condemn them is a heinous crime." Wherefore this distinction of sins against and sins besides the law falls to dust, and our minor proposition stands firm, that he who commits venial sins transgresses the law of God and is therefore unrighteous for his so doing.

Becanus here forsakes the Cardinal in this distinction, and helps him by another device. He grants that venial sins are against the law, and proves it because every venial sin is morally evil, and therefore contrary to right reason and eternal law. But here is now the distinction: It is one thing to be against the law, and another to be against the boundary of the law. All venial sins bar against the law, but no venial sin is properly against the end of the law, that is, against charity, the love of God or our neighbor. Is not this a wondrously fine invention? It is as if a subject who has in many things broken the law should say, "True, my faults are against the law of the land, but yet they are not against the end of those laws, that is, obedience to my Prince, and love for the good of him and my country. Though I break the laws, yet I would not have you think other than that I love and honor my Prince and country well enough."

Just so the Jesuits. A man may commit many sins against God's law and yet observe the end of the law in loving God with all his heart and his neighbor as himself. Nothing can be more senseless than that a man should offend God in breaking His law and yet, notwithstanding, love God with his whole heart; that a man should wrong his neighbor, doing that to him which he would not have done to himself, and yet, for all that, love his neighbor as himself.

Three Objections to the Truth Answered

"If you love Me, keep My commandments" (John 14:15), says Christ.

"No," say the Romanists, "we love Him and yet break His commandments."

"Love doeth not evil to his neighbor" (Romans 13:10), says the apostle.

"No," say the Jesuits, "love may do evil to his neighbor, and yet keep the name of love."

A man may be angry with another without cause, revile him, call him *Raca*, and defraud him in small matters (for these they make venial sins) and yet, in the meantime, all the while be without breach of charity. He would not willingly be so used, but he will use another in this way, and yet look to be thanked for his love too. Such gross absurdities our adversaries run into by coining such senseless distinctions of sins not against, but besides the law, or of sins not against the end of the law, though against the law itself.

Our consciences cannot be satisfied with such silly shifts, and therefore we leave them unto those who can content themselves to choke up their consciences with a little sophistry. These are men who make a pastime of sin, and take liberty to qualify and dispense with God's laws as they think agreeable to their consciences, hoping by tricks of wit and dodging distinctions to avoid the accusations of conscience, and to elude the severity of God's judgment.

SECTION IV

Chapter 11

Justification by works makes void the covenant of grace, the difference between the law and the gospel, the use of the law, and the erroneous thinking of our adversaries in this point

So much for these three objections to our second argument, proving the impossibility of our justification by the works of the law because we cannot perfectly fulfill the law. We go now forward unto two arguments more, one taken from the difference between the two covenants God has made with man (of works and of grace), and the other taken from the nature of true Christian liberty obtained for us by Christ's death.

Our third argument is as follows: That which makes void the covenant of grace is a false and heretical doctrine. But justification by works of the law makes void the covenant of grace. Ergo, it is false and heretical so to teach.

For confirmation of the minor premise in this argument we must briefly show what the covenant of grace and the covenant of works are, and what opposition there is between these two.

By the covenant of grace we understand simply the

Justification by Works Voids the Covenant of Grace 155

gospel, i.e., the gracious appointment of God to bring men to salvation by Jesus Christ. In the administration of this gracious purpose of God, we must observe four periods of time wherein God has presented in various forms this means of man's salvation.

The first is from Adam until Abraham. God made the promise to Adam soon after his miserable fall, and renewed it as occasion served unto the patriarchs and holy men of that first age of the world, that the seed of the woman should break the serpent's head. This blessed promise, containing the whole substance of man's redemption by Christ, was religiously accepted and embraced by the servants of God in those times. They showed their faith in it by offering sacrifices as God had taught them, and their thankfulness for it by their obedience and holy conduct.

The second period is from Abraham to Moses. After men had now almost forgotten God's promise and their own duty, and idolatry had crept into those families wherein by succession the Church of God had continued, God called forth Abraham from among his idolatrous kindred, and with him renewed that former promise in the form of a league and covenant confirmed by word and solemn ceremonies. God on the one side promised to be the God of Abraham and his seed, and that in his seed all the nations of the earth should be blessed. Abraham, for his part, believed the promise and accepted the condition of obedience, to walk before God in uprightness. This covenant with Abraham was ratified by two external ceremonies. One was a firebrand passing between the pieces of the heifer and other beasts which Abraham, according to the custom in making covenants, had divided in two (Genesis 15). The other was the sacrament of circumcision upon the flesh of Abraham and his posterity (Genesis 17).

The third period is from the time of Moses until Christ. After the Church multiplied unto a nation, and withal, in process of time and continuance among the idolatrous Egyptians, grew extremely corrupt in religion and manners, God again revised His former covenant made with Abraham. He put the Jews in remembrance of the covenant of grace in Christ first by adding unto the first sacrament of circumcision another of the Passover, setting forth unto the Jews the Author of their deliverance both from the spiritual slavery and punishment of sin and from the bodily bondage and plagues of Egypt. Afterwards God instituted various rites and ceremonies concerning priests and sacrifices, all of which were shadows of good things to come, that is, of Christ and the Church's redemption by His death. These things were prefigured through those types somewhat darkly, yet plainly enough to the weak understanding of the Jews who, in that youthful period of the Church, stood in need of such schoolmasters and tutors to direct them unto Christ.

The fourth and last period is from Christ's death to the end of the world. Christ, in the fullness of time appearing in our flesh, accomplished all the prophecies and promises that went before Him, and by the sacrifice of Himself confirmed that covenant anew which so long ago had been made with the Church. Withal, having abolished whatsoever before was weak and imperfect, He has now replenished the Church with an abundance of knowledge and grace, still to continue and increase till the consummation of all things. In all these periods of time, the grace of God that brings salvation to man was ever one and the same; only the revelation thereof was with much variety of

Justification by Works Voids the Covenant of Grace 157

circumstances, as God considered it agreeable to every season. In the first it was called a promise, in the second a covenant, in the two last periods a testament (the Old from Moses till Christ's death, the New from then to the world's end), in both remission of sins and salvation bequeathed as a legacy unto the Church. This bequest was ratified by the death of the Testator, typically slain in the sacrifices as confirmation of the old, really put to death in His own person as the sanction of the new testament. But, notwithstanding this or any other diversity in circumstance, the substance of the gospel or covenant of grace is but one and the same throughout all ages, namely Jesus Christ, yesterday and today and the same forever.

In the next place, by the covenant of works we understand that which we call the law, namely that means of bringing man to salvation which is by perfect obedience to the will of God.

Hereof there are also two separate administrations. The first is with Adam before his fall, when immortality and happiness were promised to man and confirmed by an external symbol of the tree of life, upon condition that he continued obedient to God, as well in all other things as in that particular commandment of not eating of the tree of knowledge of good and evil. The second administration of this covenant was the renewing thereof with the Israelites at Mount Sinai, where (after the light of nature had begun to grow darker, and corruption had in time worn out the characters of religion and virtue, as first engraved on man's heart) God revived the law by a compendious and full declaration of all duties required of man towards God and his neighbor, expressed in the Decalogue. According to the tenor of this law God entered into covenant with the Israelites, promising to be their God in bestowing upon them all blessings of life and happiness upon condition that they would be His people, obeying all things that He had commanded. This condition they accepted, promising an absolute obedience: "All things which the Lord hath said, we will do" (Exodus 19:8). And they also submitted themselves to all punishment in case they disobeyed, saying "Amen" to the curse of the law: "Cursed be everyone that confirmeth not all the words of this law to do them; and all the people shall say, 'Amen' " (Deuteronomy 27:26).

We see in brief what these covenants of grace and works are. Next we must inquire what opposition there is between these two: grace and works, the gospel and the law. The opposition is not in regard to the end at which both aim. They both agree in one common end, namely the glory of God in man's eternal salvation. The disagreement is in the means whereby this end may be attained, which are proposed to men in one fashion by the law, in another by the gospel.

The difference is this: The law offers life unto man upon condition of perfect obedience, cursing the transgressors thereof in the least point with eternal death. The gospel offers life unto man upon another condition, repentance and faith in Christ, promising remission of sins to such as repent and believe. That this is the main essential and proper difference between the covenant of works and of grace (that is, between the law and the gospel) we shall endeavor to make good against those of the Romish apostasy who deny it.

Let us consider then the law of works, either as given to Adam before the promise or as after the promise it remained in some force with Adam and all his posterity. For the time before man's fall, it is apparent that perfect obe-

Justification by Works Voids the Covenant of Grace

dience was the condition required for the establishing of Adam in perpetual bliss. Other means there were not, nor did any need to be proposed unto him. But when man had failed in that condition, and so broken the covenant of works, God, to repair man's ruined state, now desperate of ever attaining unto happiness by the first means, appointed a second, offering unto Adam a Savior, so that by faith in Him, and not by his own unspotted obedience, he might recover justification and the life which he had lost. What Adam should have obtained by works without Christ, now he could receive by faith in Christ without works.

Since the time of man's fall we must consider that although the law and gospel go together, yet just as they still differ in their use and office between each other, so also the law's use now differs from the use it had before the fall. For us now it does not have the same use as it had in man's innocence.

It was given to Adam to bring him to life, and for that purpose it was sufficient both in itself, as an absolute rule of perfection, and in regard to Adam, who had strength to have observed it. But unto fallen man, although the band of obedience remains, yet the end thereof, justification and life by it, is now abolished by the promise because the law is now insufficient for that purpose, not of itself, but by reason of our sinful flesh that cannot keep it. This is most manifest by the renewing of the first covenant of works with the Jews when God delivered unto them the moral law from Sinai, at which time God did not intend that the Jews should obtain salvation by obedience to the law. God promised life if they could obey, and the Jews, as was their duty, promised to obey. But God knew well enough that they were never able to keep their promise, and therefore it was not God's intention in this legal covenant with the Jews that any of them should ever attain justification and life by that means.

At first the promise did not need to have been made unto Adam, since the law could suffice for the attaining of life. So after the promise was once made, the law was not renewed with the Jews with the same purpose that righteousness and life should be gained by observing it. This is the plain doctrine of the apostle in his excellent dispute against justification by the law. The doubt that troubled the Galatians was this: God had made an evangelical covenant with Abraham (Galatians 3:8) that in Christ he and his faithful seed should be blessed, that is, justified. After 430 years He made a legal covenant with Abraham's posterity that they should live, that is, be justified and saved, if they fulfilled all things written in the law.

The question now was which of these two covenants should stand in force, or whether both could stand together. The apostle answers that the former covenant should stand in force, and that the latter did not abrogate the former, nor yet could it stand in force together with the former. This he expresses: "And this I say, that the covenant that was confirmed before of God in respect of Christ, the law, which was 430 years after, cannot disannul that it should make the promise of none effect. For if the inheritance (that is, of righteousness and life) be by the law, it is not by the promise. But God gave it to Abraham by promise. Wherefore, then, serveth the law?" (Galatians 3:17–19).

Here now they might object: "If men cannot be justified by keeping the law, to what end was it given so long after the promise was made?"

To this the apostle answers, "It was added (unto the promise) because of transgressions" (Galatians 3:19).

Justification by Works Voids the Covenant of Grace   161

Here is the true use of the moral law since the fall of man, not to justify him and give life, but to prove him to be unjust and worthy of death. It was added because of transgressions, that is:

1. To convince man of sin that he might be put in remembrance what was his duty of old, what was his present infirmity in doing it, and what was God's wrath against him for not doing it. Seeing how impossible it was for him to attain unto life by this old way of the law, first appointed in Paradise, he should be humbled and driven to look after that new way which God had, since that time, laid forth, more heedfully attending the promise and seeking Christ, who is the end of the law unto everyone who believes in Him. This use God pointed out unto the Jews, prefiguring Christ unto them in the mercy seat, which covered the ark wherein the tables of the covenant were kept, and in the sacrifices appointed for all sorts of transgressions against this covenant. To admonish the Jews, a further thing was aimed at in giving them the law, namely bringing them to Christ, the promised seed, in whom remission of sins and life eternal were to be had.

2. To restrain man from sin, that the law might be a perpetual rule of holiness and obedience whereby man should walk and glorify God to the utmost of his power. The law was given so that those Jews might not think that God, by making a gracious promise, had utterly nullified the law, and that now men might live as they pleased, but that they might know these bounds prescribed for them by God, within which compass they were to keep themselves, that the overflowing of iniquity might be restrained. These most excellent, perpetual, and necessary uses of the moral law God intended in the renewing of the legal covenant with the Jews; and therefore the apostle

concludes that God did not cross Himself when He first gave the inheritance to Abraham by promise and afterwards made a legal covenant with the Jews, his posterity. "Is the law then against the promises?" asks the apostle. "God forbid. For if there had been a law given which could have given life, surely righteousness should have been by the law. But the Scripture hath concluded all under sin, that the promise by the faith of Jesus Christ might be given to all that believe" (Galatians 3:21–22). Whence it is most clear that the law and the gospel are in some things subordinate to and uphold one another, while in others they are absolute and destroy one another.

3. As the law, by the discovery of sin and the punishment of it, humbles man and prepares him to receive the gospel; as the law is a sacred direction for holiness and obedience to those who have embraced the gospel and all others; now, third, the law requires satisfaction for the breach of it, and the gospel promises such satisfaction. Thus the law and gospel agree well together and establish one another. But as the law gives life to them who perfectly obey it, and the gospel gives life to them who steadfastly believe it, thus the law and gospel are one against each other and overthrow one another. And therefore, if God had given such a law to the Jews as could have brought salvation to them through the perfect fulfilling of it, it would be apparent that God would have made void His former covenant unto Abraham because righteousness would have been by the law and not by Christ. But now God gave no such law as could be kept by the Jews, as the apostle proves, because all were sinners against it; and therefore it follows that, notwithstanding the giving of the law, the promise stands good forever, and righteousness is to be obtained only by faith in Jesus Christ.

From hence we conclude firmly that the difference between the law and the gospel, as assigned by our divines, is most certain and agreeable to the Scriptures; that is, the the law gives life unto the just upon the condition of perfect obedience in all things, while the gospel gives life unto sinners upon the condition that they repent and believe in Christ Jesus. Whence it is plain that in the point of justification these two are incompatible, and that therefore our minor proposition stands verified: that justification by the works of the law makes void the covenant of grace. This proposition is the same as the apostle's assertion elsewhere, "If righteousness be by the law, Christ died in vain" (Galatians 2:21), and, "Ye are abolished from Christ, whosoever are justified by the law; ye are fallen from grace" (Galatians 5:4).

The claims of the Romish Church regarding the gospel of Christ are so much more injurious because, by denying this difference, they would confound the law and gospel, and bring us back from Christ to Moses to seek our justification in fulfilling the moral law. They would persuade us that the gospel is nothing but a more perfect law, or the law perfected by the addition of the Spirit enabling men to fulfill it; that the promises of the gospel are upon this condition of fulfilling the law, with such like stuff. Their doctrine on this point is declared unto us by Bellarmine, where he coins many distinctions between the law and gospel, but will by no means admit that which our reformed divines make the chief one.

The chief distinction he sees between them he frames by stating that the gospel should be taken in a double sense:

First, as the doctrine of Christ and His apostles, preached and written by them.

Second, as the grace of the Holy Ghost given in the New Testament, which He makes to be the law written in our hearts, that quickening Spirit, the law of faith, charity shed abroad in our hearts, in opposition to the law written in stone, the dead and killing letter, the law of works, the spirit of bondage and fear.

Upon this basis he proceeds to the difference between the law and the gospel, thus: The law teaches us what is to be done; the gospel (if it is taken to represent the grace of the Holy Ghost) differs from the law because it gives strength to do it; but if it is taken for the doctrine delivered by Christ and His apostles, so it agrees with the law, teaching us as the law does what things are to be done. This argument the Jesuit illustrates and proves in three particulars:

First, the gospel contains the doctrine of works, or the law. For the moral precepts of the gospel are the same as those in the law, even those precepts that seem most evangelical, such as loving our enemies. Through all the writings of the New Testament we find precepts and exhortations to the same virtues, and prohibitions from the same vices which the law forbids or commands. So that as for morals, the doctrine of the gospel is but the doctrine of the law, newly, that is, most clearly and fully expounded. Nor is the gospel more perfect in substance, but in circumstance a more perspicuous doctrine.

This argument, though true, is yet very ridiculously proved by the Cardinal out of Matthew 5:20: "Unless your righteousness exceeds (What? He says not the righteousness of the law and prophets, but) that of the scribes and Pharisees, ye shall not enter the kingdom of heaven." Bellarmine suggests that Christ would not add to the burden of the law, but does so in order to take away from the false gloss of the scribes and Pharisees. Surely our Savior had good cause to fault both the doctrine of the Pharisees in interpreting the law and their hypocritical practice of the law in outward matters without inward obedience. But there was no reason for Christ to require of man more perfection than God's law required, and it is a fancy to dream of any such meaning in our Savior's speech.

Second, the gospel contains condemnations and threats as the law does. Witness the many woes from Christ's own mouth against the scribes and Pharisees, together with those frequent declarations of judgment and damnation against such as are ungodly, who do not repent and obey the gospel.

Third, the gospel contains promises of life and happiness, but these evangelical promises are not absolute, but upon the same condition as the legal ones, that is, with the condition of fulfilling the law through actual and laborious righteousness, which consists in the perfect observation of the commandments. This the Jesuit would prove unto us:

- From Matthew 5: "Unless your righteousness abounds (that is, in Bellarmine's construction, so far as) unto the perfect keeping of the law, you shall not enter the kingdom of heaven."

- From Matthew 19:17 and Mark 10:19, where Christ speaks to the young man who asked Him what he should do to be saved: "If thou wilt enter into life, keep the commandments." And to the lawyer who asked the same question He answers, "This do and thou shalt live" (Luke 10:28). That is, fulfill the law, and you shall be saved. In these places they say that Christ preached the gospel and showed these men the very evangelical way to salvation.

- From the many passages of Scripture where mortification of sin and the studious practice of holiness and obedience are required of us. "If ye mortify the deeds of the flesh by the Spirit, ye shall live" (Romans 8:13). "If the wicked will return from all his sins that he hath committed, and keep all My statutes, and do that which is lawful and right, he shall surely live and not die" (Ezekiel 18:21).

• From the very tenor of the gospel: "He that believeth shall be saved . . . but he that believeth not shall be damned" (Mark 16:16). "If ye know those things, happy are ye if ye do them" (John 13:17). "Ye are my friends, if ye do whatsoever I command you" (John 15:14). Here we see that the promise of life is not absolute, but conditional, that we do such and such works.

From hence the Romanist concludes that, since the precepts, threats, and promises of the gospel are substantially the same as those of the law, the true difference between the law and gospel is this: The law nakedly proposes what is to be done without giving grace to perform it, while the gospel not only proposes what is to be done, but withal gives grace and strength to do it. And therefore the law given by Moses the lawgiver cannot justify because it was given without the grace to fulfill it; but the gospel given by Christ the Redeemer does justify because it is accompanied by the grace of the Holy Ghost, making us able to keep the law. For this cause also the law of Moses is an unsupportable yoke, the law of fear and bondage (Romans 8:15; Galatians 4:24–25), because it gives no grace to keep it, but only convinces us of our sin and threatens our punishment. But the law of Christ, the gospel, is a light yoke, a law of love and liberty, because it gives grace to keep it and to render love to God and man, and therefore frees a man from feared punishment.

This is the sum of the Romish doctrine concerning the

Justification by Works Voids the Covenant of Grace

difference between the moral law and the gospel in the point of justification, as it is delivered to us by Bellarmine, the rotten pillar of the anti-christian synagogue. Wherein we have scarcely a syllable of distinct truth, but all is perverted by equivocations and gross ambiguities, as shall appear by a short survey of the former discourse. Where he distinguishes the gospel into two items, the doctrine of Christ and His apostles and the grace of the Holy Ghost, let us follow him in these two parts, the first of which will occupy the remainder of this chapter:

First, as for doctrine, we grant that the gospel is often so taken; but in this matter about justification this meaning is too large and not distinct enough. For although, by a synecdoche of the chief and most excellent part, the whole doctrine and ministry of Christ and His apostles with their successors is called the doctrine of the gospel and the ministry of the gospel—"At that day when God shall judge the secrets of men by Jesus Christ according to my gospel" (Romans 12:16)—yet all things which they preached or wrote are not the gospel properly so called. But as Moses chiefly delivered the law unto the Jews, nevertheless also he wrote of Christ, and so in part revealed unto them the gospel. So Christ and His ministers, though chiefly they preach the gospel, yet also present the law in its place having a singular use in furthering our Christian faith and practice. Wherefore, when we speak of the gospel as opposite to the law, it is a Jesuitical equivocation to take it in this large sense. As for the whole doctrine preached by Christ and His apostles, and written for us in the books of the New Testament, we follow the apostle in this dispute over justification (Galatians 3:4–5). And according as he takes the gospel strictly here as meaning the promise of justification and life made unto man in Christ

Jesus, this is in proper terms the gospel, that special doctrine concerning man's redemption and reconciliation with God by the means of Jesus Christ—the revelation whereof was indeed the gladdest tidings that were ever brought to the ear of mortal man.

This gospel in strict terms the angels preached. "Behold, I bring you glad tidings of great joy, which shall be to all people. For unto you is born this day in the city of David a Savior, which is Christ the Lord" (Luke 2:10–11). And afterwards, Christ and His apostles fully explained the mysteries thereof unto the world. According to this necessary distinction, we answer that if we take the gospel in that large meaning, what Bellarmine has said is true, that the gospel contains in it the doctrine of works, the moral law, even the very same precepts, prohibitions, threats, and promises which are delivered in the law. Christ and His apostles preached all these things, and so may all ministers without blame; yea, they must, if they will avoid blame, press the same upon their hearers seasonably and discreetly, that the law may make way for the better receiving and entertainment of grace in the gospel. But it does not follow that the gospel properly so taken is to be confounded as one and the same thing with the law, just because the law is conjoined with it in the preaching and writings of the ministers of the New Testament. They still are divided in their nature and offices, nor has the gospel any affinity with the law in its precepts, threats, or promises. Wherefore, when Bellarmine teaches us that evangelical promises are made with the condition of perfectly fulfilling the law, it is a desperate error, and that in its very foundation. You heard his proofs recited before; see now how extremely weak they are.

1. Matthew 5: "Except your righteousness . . . ." To this

Justification by Works Voids the Covenant of Grace

we answer that the plain meaning is this: "Our righteousness must abound more than that of the Pharisees, that is, it must not be on the outside only as theirs was, but inward as well as of the outward action, or else such hypocrisy will keep us from entering into heaven." But does it hence follow that, because we must be more perfect than these Pharisees, therefore we must be as perfect as the law in all things requires, or that exceeding them means equaling the holiness of the law in all points? Because we must be sincere without hypocrisy, therefore must we be perfect in all things without blame? Such consequences as these the Jesuit has concluded out of his own head, not out of the text.

2. Regarding those words of Christ to the young man (Matthew 19), and the lawyer (Luke 10), that if they fulfilled the law they should live, we answer that Christ, in so speaking unto them, did not preach the gospel, but showed unto them the legal way to salvation. For these err, committing that grand error of the Jew in seeking for righteousness not by faith but by the works of the law, severing the law from Christ the end thereof (as the apostle shows in Romans 9:31–32; 10:3), and so supposing that they can be saved by doing some good thing. Christ answers them in their own kind, as everyone should be answered who swells with high conceits of his own righteousness and works, that there was a law to be kept, and that if they could fully observe the righteousness of it they would be saved. He thus sends them purposely to the law that they might be humbled thereby and see their great folly in seeking for life by that which they were so unable to keep. Against this answer the Jesuit has nothing to reply, but spends much time confuting another answer made by some of our divines, namely that Christ spoke

these things ironically. This Bellarmine seeks to confute, nor do I labor to confirm it, though it might be justified against anything he brings to the contrary.

3. As for those places of Scripture that promise life, blessedness, and the favor of God upon condition of holiness in life and conduct—that we mortify the lusts of the flesh, walk in the Spirit, and overcome the world, we answer that obedience is one thing, but perfect obedience is another. We say that the promises of the gospel are all upon condition of obedience, but none upon condition of perfect obedience. It is an injurious misrepresentation of us when they say that we teach that evangelical promises are absolute and without condition, as if God promised and gives all to us, and we must do nothing for it on our part. We defend no such dotage. The promises of the gospel are conditional, namely upon condition of repentance and amendment of life. We must seek, to the extent of our power, to obey God in all things, but this is such a condition as requires of us sincerity and faithfulness of endeavor, not perfection of obedience in the full performance of every jot and tittle of the law.

4. Unto the last argument from the tenor of the New Covenant, that we must believe if we will be saved, and therefore the promise of the gospel depends upon the condition of fulfilling the law—this is an argument which might make the Cardinal's cheek as red as his cap, were there any shame in him. Faith indeed is a work, and this work is required as a condition of the promise; but to do this work of believing, though it is to obey God's commandment, yet is not perfectly fulfilling the whole law, but perfectly trusting in Him who brings mercy and pardon for transgressions of the law.

Chapter 12

*Bellarmine's erroneous distinction
of the word "gospel"*

So much for the first half of the Jesuit's distinction wherein his sophistic fraud appears, taking the gospel to mean the whole doctrine of the New Testament published by Christ and His apostles, and therefore confounding the law and the gospel as one because he finds the law as well as the gospel delivered unto us by our Savior and His ministers. I proceed to the second branch of his distinction.

The gospel, he says, is also taken for the grace of the Holy Ghost given to us in the New Testament period whereby men are made able to keep the law. But where is it so taken? The Jesuit cannot tell you that. For he says, "I affirm that I am using the word 'gospel' accurately truly, because there is no place in the Scripture where the word is used other than to signify teaching." There is no good reason for him to give this definition, inasmuch as it is evident to all men that there is great difference between the doctrine of man's salvation by the mercy of God through the merits of Christ (which is properly the gospel) and the graces of the Holy Ghost bestowed on man in his regeneration whereby he is made able in some measure to do that which is good. But the fault is not so much in calling the grace of God in us by the name of the gospel as in the misinterpretation of the matter itself. Wherein he commits two errors:

1. He makes the grace of the New Testament age to be such strength given to man that he may fulfill the law.

2. He says the law was given without grace to keep it.

In both assertions there is ambiguity and error. First, we grant that grace to do anything that is good is given by the gospel, not by the law. The law commands, but it gives no strength to obey, because it presupposes that he to whom the command is given has or ought to have already in himself strength to obey it. And therefore we confess freely that we receive the Spirit not by the works of the law, but by the hearing of faith preached (Galatians 3:2). The donation of the Spirit in any measure whatsoever of His sanctifying graces is from Christ as a Savior, not as a Lawgiver.

Thus, then, we agree that all grace to do well is given unto us by the gospel, but we differ in that they teach that the gospel gives such grace unto man that he may fulfill what the law commands and so be justified by it. We deny this and say that grace is given by the gospel to obey the law sincerely without hypocrisy, but not to fulfill it perfectly without infirmities. In this point the Jesuit fails in the proofs which he brings.

He fails in interpreting those passages where contrary attributes are ascribed to the law and the gospel. The law is described as the ministry of death and condemnation (2 Corinthians 3:7), a killing letter (2 Corinthians 3:6), working wrath (Romans 4:15; 1 Corinthians 15:56), a yoke of bondage (Galatians 5:1), and a testament bringing forth children unto bondage (Galatians 4:24). But the gospel is the ministry of life (2 Corinthians 3:6) and of reconciliation (2 Corinthians 5:19), the Spirit that quickens (2 Corinthians 3:6; 7:17; Galatians 4:26), and the testament bringing forth children to liberty. This opposition

Bellarmine's Erroneous Distinction

Bellarmine acknowledges, saying that the law gives precepts without affording strength to keep them, but the gospel gives grace to do what is commanded.

But the Jesuit is here mistaken. These opposite attributes given to the law are ascribed to it in a twofold respect. First, they are in regard to the punishment which the law threatens for offenders: death. In this regard principally the law is said to be the ministry of death, to work wrath, to be not a dead but a killing letter—inasmuch as, being broken, it leaves no hope for the transgressor, but a fearful expectation of eternal death and condemnation of the law, under the terrors whereof it holds them in bondage. But, on the contrary, the gospel is the ministry of life, of reconciliation, of the quickening Spirit, and of liberty because it reveals unto us Christ in whom we are restored to life from the deserved death and condemnation of the law. Through the gospel we regain God's favor, being delivered from the wrath to come unto liberty, being freed from slavish fear of punishment. This is the chief reason for this opposition of attributes.

Second, the next aspect of this opposition is in regard to obedience. In this respect the ministry of the law is said to be the ministry of the letter, written on tables of stone. But that of the gospel is called the ministry of the Spirit which writes the law on the fleshly tables of the heart. The law commands, but gives or administers no power to obey, and so is but as a dead letter without the virtue of the Spirit. But in the gospel grace is given from Christ, who by the Holy Ghost sanctifies the heart of His elect that they may live to righteousness—in a sincere thought, not in exact conformity in every way to the law of God.

We will give a similar answer to another proof presented by the Jesuit, where he says that the law came by

Moses without grace to fulfill it, but grace to keep it comes by Christ. "The law came by Moses, but grace and truth by Jesus Christ" (John 1:17). We answer that the true interpretation of these words is this: Moses delivered a twofold law, moral and ceremonial. Opposite to these, Christ has brought a twofold privilege. First, He brings grace for the moral law, whereby we understand not only the power given to the regenerate to observe in part this law (which strength could not come by the law itself), but also much more remission of sins committed against the law—and so our justification and freedom from the guilt of sin and curse of the moral law. Second, Christ brings truth for the ceremonial law, the substance being brought in and the shadows having vanished.

Wherefore the Jesuit errs greatly in this point when he makes the grace of the New Testament to consist in the fact that strength is thereby given us to fulfill the law. The grace of God in the gospel is chiefly our justification and redemption from the curse of the law, along with strength afforded us to obey the law in some measure, though not perfectly as our adversaries would have it.

In the next point, he errs as much in saying that the law of Moses was given without grace to obey it. This is false, for, although the law itself did not give grace, it is certain that grace was given by Christ even when Moses published the law. It is sufficient proof that, first, these excellent properties are ascribed unto the law of God, especially in the Psalms, such as Psalms 19 and 119, where the law of God is said to give light to the eyes, to convert the soul, and to make the heart rejoice, which it could not do of itself had not the grace of the Holy Ghost been given in these times, without which the law could work no such saving effects.

Second, consider the experience of the faithful in those times—the patience, obedience, and all sorts of graces shining in those ancient saints who lived before and after the law was given. This grace they received from the Holy Ghost, shed upon their hearts by virtue of Christ's mediation, whereby they received strength to live in holy obedience to the law of God.

The difference between these times and those under the law is not that we have grace and they had none, but only in the measure and extent of the same grace bestowed both on us and on them. In those times, as the doctrine of the gospel was more obscurely revealed, so the grace which accompanied it was more sparingly distributed, being confined to a Church collected of one nation and bestowed upon that Church in a lesser measure than now, though yet sufficiently in that measure. But in the times of the New Testament, the light shines more brightly and grace is dispensed more liberally, being extended impartially to all nations, and poured upon all the godly in a larger abundance, just as was promised in Jeremiah 31 (though also this comparison must be considered in general, not with regard to every individual, for no doubt, in many particulars, some men under the law exceed, in abundance of grace, many under the gospel). Wherefore it is a notable injury unto the bounty of God and the honor of those saints of old to exclude them from partaking in the gospel; to affirm that they were led only by the spirit of fear and not of love; to claim that they did not receive the spirit of adoption to cry "Abba, Father" as well as we (though not as fully as we); and to conclude therefore that they were not sons, though they were under tutors and governors. We confess that they were like servants held in bondage, excluded from the inheritance of grace and glory till after Christ's death. But it is wrong to claim that their adoption was but conditional with regard to the time to come, and to speak of them as if they were handled as slaves fearing temporal punishments, allured by temporal rewards like a herd of swine, fed with base acorns and husks.

These are absurd errors bred out of Scripture misunderstood, especially that of John 1:17 ("grace came by Christ," and therefore not before Christ's incarnation). This is a silly argument. Christ is as old as the world and His grace is as ancient as the name of man upon the earth. Grace always came by Christ, and was in a measure given by Him long before He appeared in the flesh. He was ever the head of His Church, and that was His body, which He always quickened by the blessed influence of His Spirit ministering thereunto. Whereby the godly before as well as since His incarnation were made living members of His mystical body. Wherefore it is apparent that grace is not to be tied to the times of the gospel and severed from the law. No, just as of old the law was not always without grace, so many times the gospel itself is without grace, Christ Himself being a stumbling stone and a rock of offense, and the gospel is a savor of death to many of those upon whom grace is not bestowed to believe and embrace it.

I conclude, then, that this difference which our adversaries make between the law and gospel is false, and that their error is pernicious in making the gospel to be nothing but the Spirit added to the law so that man may fulfill it to his justification, and so that a man may be saved by Christ through the perfect fulfilling of the law. This is a monstrous and uncouth doctrine, laying an unsupportable burden upon the conscience of man and exposing his soul to eternal destruction. By this means he frustrates the graces of God in Christ, and withal frustrates his own hopes of life, expecting to obtain it by that law which he is never able to fulfill.

SECTION V

Chapter 13

Justification by fulfilling the law overthrows Christian liberty

So much for the third argument. The last one is drawn from the nature of Christian liberty: that which overthrows our Christian liberty, purchased for us by the death of Christ, is no evangelical doctrine, but a heretical one. But justification by the works of the law overthrows the spiritual liberty of man obtained for him by Christ. Ergo, it is a heresy against the gospel.

For the proof of the minor proposition, let us in brief consider wherein stands that liberty wherewith Christ has made us free, so that we may better perceive what part thereof this doctrine of justification by works nullifies and takes from us. The liberty we have in Christ is either in regard to the life to come or to this present life. The first is the liberty of glory, consisting in a full deliverance from the state of vanity and misery, both sinful and painful, whereunto we are now subject; "and not we only, but the whole creation which with us groans and travails in pain, till with us it also shall be delivered from the bondage of corruption into the glorious liberty of the sons of God" (Romans 8:21–23). This liberty we have in hope, not in

Justification by the Law Overthrows Liberty

possession. The next we actually enjoy in this life, and that is the liberty of grace. This one we may divide not unfitly into three branches: freedom from sin, freedom from the law, and freedom from men.

1. Our freedom from sin stands in two things. First is our deliverance from the punishment of sin. For every sin in its own nature brings with it guilt and a sure obligation unto punishment, binding over the transgressor unto the pains of God's eternal wrath by a stronger chain than of steel or silver. Christ, by His meritorious satisfaction, has broken these bonds, and ransomed us from this fearful bondage unto hell and destruction. He, being made a curse for us, has "redeemed us from the curse of the law" (Galatians 3:13). That is, by taking on Himself the punishment for our sins in His own person, suffering and satisfying the wrath and justice of God, He has forever set us free from the dreadful vengeance of God, which we deserve to receive upon us for our iniquities.

Second, our freedom from sin stands in our deliverance from the power of sin, which, though it abides in us in the relics of our corrupted nature, yet (by the power of the Holy Ghost dwelling in the hearts of the regenerate) is subdued and kept under so that it does not reign nor exercise its commanding authority without control. So whereas the unregenerate are the servants of sin, wholly at the command of Satan and wicked affections, the regenerate are freed from this slavery, being ruled and guided by the Spirit of the Lord which, wheresoever it is, gives liberty (2 Corinthians 3:17). The liberty is from that blindness wherein we are held by nature, not knowing what is the will of God. That liberty is also from that rebellion and infirmity of our nature, whereby we are not willing, nor able to do the will of God—from which we are freed in part by the Spirit of Christ, enlightening our minds and changing our hearts.

This liberty from sin's dominion and damnation, St. Paul joins together: "The law of the Spirit of life, which is in Christ Jesus, hath freed me from the law of sin and of death" (Romans 8:2). "Sin shall not have dominion over you, for ye are not under the law, but under grace" (Romans 6:14).

2. Our freedom from the law is from either the ceremonial or the moral law. The ceremonial law contains in it various carnal ordinances to endure until the time of reformation, from this law Christ has freed the church of the New Testament.

First, we are freed from the whole burden of all the legal ceremonies used in the worship of God (Hebrews 9:19–21). Those resemblances are of no use now that the substance itself has come, nor may such beggarly and impotent rudiments be sought after when greater perfection is to be had (Galatians 4:9).

Second, the church is freed from that restraint in things indifferent whereunto the Jews were tied, but we are not bound. Such are the observations of days, of meats and drinks, of garments, and the like, wherein the Jews were restrained but our consciences are left free, being taught that every creature of God is good, being sanctified by prayer and thanksgiving (1 Timothy 4:4–5), and that "to the pure, all things are pure" (Titus 1:15). Only this must be observed, that we do not abuse our liberty, but that as we are informed by faith that all things are lawful for us, so we should be taught by charity to see what is expedient in regard to others, so that a due regard is had for others' infirmity (1 Corinthians 10:23) and that nothing is done whereby the truly weak may be scandalized (Romans

14:21). By this means knowledge on the one side still preserves us, so that our consciences are not ensnared with superstition, and charity on the other side keeps our liberty from degenerating into licentiousness and unchristian contempt of our brethren.

Our freedom from the moral law stands in this: that the law requires of every man, upon strictest terms of necessity, full and complete obedience to all things contained in it if he would avoid the punishment of hell fire; but Christ has freed all who believe in Him from this heavy and rigorous exaction of the law, taking away from our consciences this obligation to fulfill it upon pain that we shall forfeit heaven if we do it not, as we shall soon see.

3. In the last place, our freedom is free from men, namely from all power and authority they may claim over our consciences. They may hold our persons in subjection, but they cannot command our consciences. We acknowledge no jurisdiction of man or angel over our consciences, but only that of God who created us and Christ who has redeemed us. Whosoever therefore shall impose upon man any human traditions, opinions, or ordinations whatsoever, to tie his conscience unto obedience by virtue of his own authority—such a one treads upon God's high prerogative and usurps tyrannically over the souls of men, according as at this day that man of sin does. This liberty from human constitutions binding the conscience is properly not a benefit purchased for us by Christ's death, but a privilege of our creation whereby our consciences are exempt from men's command and subject only to God's jurisdiction. Yet, because this liberty is a part of our spiritual liberty, it is usually called Christian liberty.

But here we must observe that human constitutions are either ecclesiastical or political. Ecclesiastical constitutions concern either the matter and substance of God's worship, when anything is invented by man and commanded wherein and whereby to worship God, or the manner and external order of God's worship in the determination of indifferent circumstances tending to decency and comeliness.

As for the former, we renounce and reject all human authority whatsoever that shall, without warrant from the Scriptures, prescribe unto the Church any doctrine to be received as a divine truth or custom, ceremony, or practice to be observed as a proper art of God's most holy worship. Our Reformed churches have happily recovered their liberty by breaking asunder those cords and casting away that yoke of false doctrine, of superstitious, ceremonial will-worship wherewith not Christ, but antichrist had ensnared and oppressed the Church. And they have God's own warrant for so doing, where Isaiah 29:13 is ratified and explained by Christ: "In vain they worship Me, teaching for doctrine men's precepts" (Matthew 15:9). It was a thing contrary to God's express commandment: "Walk ye not in the statute of your fathers, neither observe their judgments, nor defile yourselves with their idols. I am the Lord your God; walk in My statutes, and keep My judgments and do them" (Ezekiel 20:18–19).

As for the latter, namely human constitutions concerning indifferent circumstances in God's worship tending to orderly decency, agreeable to the simplicity and purity of the gospel: Herein we must acknowledge the authority of the Church, not over our consciences to bind them, but over our practices to order and limit them. Accordingly, as also we do in the other branch of human obedience (that is, political or civil, comprising all law made for the governance of kingdoms or inferior states by the supreme mag-

Justification by the Law Overthrows Liberty

istrate who has authority so to do), we must be subject, "not because of wrath only, but also for conscience sake" (Romans 13:5). For the sake of conscience, not because the highest monarch on earth has power over the conscience of his meanest subject to bind it by virtue of his own authority, but because God established the magistrate's authority and commanded subjects to give obedience in lawful things. Therefore we cannot disobey them without breach of conscience in disobeying and violating God's commandment as well. But otherwise, as for any immediate power of the conscience to restrain the inward liberty thereof, no man may, without presumption, arrogate it, nor may any without slavish baseness yield to another, as the apostle commands: "Ye are bought with a price; be not ye servants of men" (1 Corinthians 7:23).

This is in brief the doctrine of Christian liberty or spiritual liberty, which we call Christian from the cause of it (Christ), by whose purchase we enjoy it, and from the subject of it (Christians) in opposition to the Jews. They did not have this liberty in all parts of it as we have, namely in freedom from the ceremonial law and from restraint in things indifferent. In all other parts they, in their measure, were freed by Christ as well as we. Again, we call it spiritual in opposition to civil and bodily liberty, because it consists of the freedom of soul and conscience, not of the freedom of the outward man. The bondage and subjection of outward freedom is not impeachment of this spiritual freedom, as Anabaptist libertines would persuade the world, contrary to the apostle's decision. "He that is called in the Lord, being a servant, is the Lord's free man" (1 Corinthians 7:22).

Chapter 14

Justification by works subjects us to the rigor and curse of the law

We are now, in the next place, to see which branch of our liberty is cut off by the doctrine of justification by works. We will not meddle with others to which it gives a back-blow, but will deal with that which it directly strikes at. We say it destroys our liberty from the moral law, which stands in that we are not obliged unto the perfect fulfilling of that law upon pain of eternal damnation if we do not, yhis gracious liberty Christ has enfranchised us with, whosoever believes in Him. And they who now teach that we are justified by the works of the law rob our consciences of this heavenly freedom, bringing us again under that miserable bondage unto the law wherein all men are held who are in the state of infidelity and unregeneration, from whom the law in its most extreme rigor exacts perfect obedience if they want to be saved.

To demonstrate this point, in the first place it is manifest that he who would be justified by the works of the law is necessarily tied to fulfilling the whole law, since it is impossible that the law should justify those who transgress it. In the next place, then, we must prove that for a man's conscience to be thus tied to the fulfilling of the law in order to obtain justification is an insupportable yoke of spiritual bondage, contrary to that liberty wherewith Christ has made every believer free. This shall appear as we confirm the following proposition: A regenerate man, endued with true faith in Christ Jesus, is not bound in conscience to fulfill the whole law for his justification.

This proposition seems very strange unto our adversaries, and to be nothing else but a ground or platform whereon to build all licentiousness and libertinism, as if we discharged men of all allegiance to God and subjection to His laws. But their calumnies are not sufficient confutations of orthodox doctrine. To stop their mouths we throw them the following distinction, whereon they may gnaw till they break their teeth before they break it in pieces. Man's conscience stands bound to the law of God in a twofold obligation:

1. Of obedience, that according to the measure of grace received he must endeavor to the utmost of his power to live conformably to the law of God in all things.

2. Of fulfilling the law, that in every jot and tittle he must observe all things whatsoever that it commands, upon pain of everlasting condemnation for the least transgression.

We teach that no true believer is freed from the obligation unto obedience, but, so far as by grace given to him he is enabled, he ought to strive to the utmost to perform all duties towards God and man commanded in the law, if he would justify his faith to be found without hypocrisy. And therefore our doctrine is no doctrine of licentiousness.

But on the other hand we teach that every believer is freed from that obligation to fulfill the law in order to attain life and justification by it. This material difference, essential to our doctrine, is not observed (or rather is suppressed) by Bellarmine, causing the Jesuit to labor much in a needless dispute to prove against us that a Christian man is tied to the observation of the moral law. He tells us that Christ is a Lawgiver as well as a Redeemer of His Church, prescribing orders for all in common, and for each one in particular. He is a Judge who sentences according to law. He is a King who rules over subjects by a law. Christ by His coming did not destroy, but fulfilled the law, expounded it, and enjoined it to be observed by us. His apostles urge it in every epistle. A Christian man sinning offends against the law, and therefore is bound to keep the law. In all this the Jesuit encounters his own fantasy and not our doctrine, which is not wounded by such misguided weapons. For we grant without disputing that every Christian is tied to observing the moral law, and we aver that it is a most unchristian and Jesuitical slander to affirm (as he does) that we teach that the Christian is liable to no law, and is subject in conscience only to the very presence of God. No, we teach that he is bound to obey to the utmost of his power, and from this obligation no authority of man or angel, pope or devil can discharge him. So much we grant that the arguments alleged by the Cardinal do prove, and nothing else. They prove that obedience is necessary to a believing Christian, but they can never prove that perfect fulfilling of the law is necessarily required of him. From this heavy burden Christ has eased the shoulders of all who are in Him by a lively faith, of whom God no longer exacts perfect obedience to His law in those strict and rigorous terms so that they should be accursed if they do not fulfill it.

This we prove by these Scriptures:

"Stand fast in the liberty wherein Christ hath made us free, and be not entangled again with the yoke of bondage" (Galatians 5:1). But what is this yoke of bondage? Is it only the observation of the ceremonial law?

No, that was indeed part of the yoke which the apostles sought to lay on the consciences of the Galatians; but it was the least and the lightest part. The weightiest burden was the fulfilling of the moral law, whereunto by the doctrine of the false apostles the Galatians stood obliged. This is plain by the text in the following words: "Behold I, Paul, say unto you that if you be circumcised, Christ shall profit you nothing. For I testify again to every man that is circumcised, that he is bound to keep the whole law" (Galatians 5:2–3). The apostle's dispute is here evident. The Galatians may not be circumcised, nor observe the ceremonial law. Why? Because if they did, Christ should not profit them at all. But what reason is there for this, that circumcision and the ceremonies should frustrate the benefit of Christ's death? The apostle alleges a good reason, because the observation of the ceremonial law tied them also to the fulfilling of the whole moral law.

The argument is thus framed: They who are bound to keep the whole law have no profit at all by Christ. But they who are circumcised are bound to keep the whole law. Ergo, those who are circumcised have no profit at all in Christ.

The minor premise in this argument is the express words of the text, and the proof of it is evident in reason, because the retaining of legal ceremonies did in effect abolish Christ's coming in the flesh, who by His coming in the flesh had abolished them. And therefore, they who in reviving them denied Christ's death had no means at all to be saved but only by fulfilling the moral law, whereunto they were necessarily bound if they meant not to perish. This reason yet is of no force before Christ's coming, and therefore, then, circumcision and other legal ceremonies did not lay upon the Jews a strict obligation to fulfill the whole law.

The major proposition is the very reason of the apostle's reflection: Men circumcised are bound to keep the whole law, and therefore Christ shall not profit them. The reason for the consequence is the proposition that if anyone is bound to keep the whole law, Christ profits that person nothing at all. This argument, and the reason thereof, will hardly pass with approbation in the Jesuit schools. "No," they will reply, "that is a *non sequitur*. For by that doctrine Christ's death has canceled that strict obligation of fulfilling the law. But everyone who believes the promise of salvation in Christ is yet notwithstanding obliged to fulfill the whole moral law." For this is, they say, the very condition whereupon he must have benefit by the promise, even perfect observation of the commandments. And therefore he is so far from being freed by Christ from this obligation unto the law, that certainly, unless he fulfills it, he shall never be saved, as Bellarmine peremptorily and bloodily determines. These men, when they wish, are wondrously merciful towards sinners, and can teach them tricks by very easy means to merit heaven and remission of sins. But their cruelty betrays their kindness in other matters, inasmuch as, when all is said and done, a sinner is driven to this: If he would be saved by Christ he must, as he is bound, perfectly keep the whole law or else there is no hope for him.

This is cold comfort for the poor believer, but happily we do not have Jesuits or Pharaoh's taskmasters set over us to exact the whole quota of bricks, but a Jesus who has freed our souls from this bitter kingdom and delivered us from the power of these rigorous and strict commands of the law. We believe an apostle of Christ against all the sycophants of Rome, and tell them that they make the

Holy Ghost to lie when they teach that in believers the obligation to keep the whole law still stands in full force and virtue, and is not discharged by the death of Christ. That is directly contrary to this argument of the apostle: "Ye are bound to keep the whole law, and therefore Christ shall not profit you."

Whence we argue thus: Whosoever is bound to keep the whole law, to such Christ is unprofitable. But unto true believers Christ is not unprofitable. Ergo, true believers are not bound to keep the whole law.

This is a conclusion most certain, as from these irrefutable premises, so also from most evident reason. For if such as believe in Christ, and who through the Spirit wait for the hope of righteousness through faith (Galatians 5:5), are yet bound to fulfill the whole law for their justification, to what end is it to believe in Christ unto righteousness and justification? If when all is done we must be saved by doing, what profit comes by believing? Can the conscience find any benefit and comfort at all in Christ if we come to the woeful conclusion that, notwithstanding that there is in Scripture much talk of faith, of Christ, of promises, and of grace, yet all this will bring us no commodity unless a further condition is performed, namely that we perfectly keep the law of God? More than anything in the world, this is to imprison the soul in wretched slavery, and to lay the conscience upon the rack of continual terrors, if heaven is not to be had but upon such hard terms.

And this is most apparently to frustrate all benefit of Christ, of promise, of faith, of grace, and of the whole work of redemption, since in the final analysis it is by the law that we must live and not by faith. The perfect fulfilling of the law must make us righteous in God's sight, and not our believing in Christ that we may be justified. For he who keeps the whole law is thereby righteous, and no one else. Here it is but a bare shift to say that, though we are bound to fulfill the law, yet Christ profits us because He gives us grace to perform our bond in exact obedience. This evasion might stand good if St. Paul were indeed finally confuted as a weak disputant. But the error of this claim has been covered before, and if nothing else were said this apostolic argument is sufficient to refute it. I proceed to other Scriptures.

"We know that the law is good, if a man use it lawfully; knowing this, that the law is not made for a righteous man, but for the lawless and disobedient, for the ungodly, for sinners, for the unholy and profane" (1 Timothy 1:8–9). The law is not given to the righteous. How must this be understood? Is it not given with respect to a distinction, as a rule prescribing what is to be done and what is not to be done? Yes, we all agree in that. How is it then not given? One answer is that it is not given to compel or condemn—as it compels to obedience, and curses the transgressors; in this fashion it is not given to the just. This answer is full of ambiguity, and needs some explication that we may know what is the compelling force of the law from which the just are freed. In the unfolding of this our adversaries and we differ. Whether we are in the right, we shall see by considering both of our interpretations. They say that the law has no coercive or compelling power over the just because the just obey it freely, with pleasure, quickly, and from the compulsion of love, that is, willingly out of love. But it has a compulsive force over the unjust, because they they are recalcitrant and must be compelled to due obedience; that is, they obey unwillingly, being forced to it by terrors and threats. And therefore, the law rules not over

Justification by Works Subjects Us to the Law

the just as servants who obey out of fear, but over sons who obey out of love.

We expound it otherwise. The law has no coercive power over the just because the just (that is, true believers in Christ Jesus) are freed from the necessity of perfectly fulfilling it in order to obtain salvation. But the law has a coercive power over the unjust and unbelievers because they are obliged unto the perfect fulfilling thereof, or else they are to be certainly accursed. And, therefore, we say the law commands over the just as over sons, requiring of them a faithful and willing endeavor; but it commands over the unjust as over servants of whom it exacts the uttermost farthing, and upon the legal default thereof threatens eternal damnation.

The difference, then, between them and us is this: They make the compulsion of the law consist in the manner or quality of man's obedience to it. It compels when men obey unwillingly. We make the compulsion of the law consist in the quality of the command and condition whereupon obedience is required. The law, then, compels when it exacts full obedience upon penalty precisely threatened to the disobedient. Here the truth is manifestly on our side. For it is plain that compulsion in a law must be taken in opposition to direction, not persuasion; for law does not persuade, but rather commands. For, if we speak properly, a law cannot be said to compel those to whom it is given, as if by any real or physical operation it forced them into obedience. It proposes what is to be done, and it sets before a man the punishment for disobedience, but it does not work on the will of man, to force it one way or the other. Wherefore, if we know in what direction a law is, we shall soon know what compulsion is.

Direction (as all agree) is the bare prescription of what is to be done or left undone. Compulsion is the exaction of obedience upon penalty to be inflicted. So a king is under the direction, not the compulsion, of the law because he is not tied to the penalty. What other coercive force there is in a law no man can imagine.

Well, then, to apply this, the just are under the direction of the law, but not under compulsion. This must of necessity be understood thus: The just are not under the coercive power of God's law because it does not exact of them full obedience upon penalty of eternal death, to be otherwise inflicted on them, as it does exact of the unjust. For otherwise there would be no difference between the just and the unjust in regard to this coercive power of the law, if both the one and the other are obliged to yield alike perfect obedience upon the like penalty. In this case the law would be as coercive to one as to the other, exacting equal obedience upon equal terms, both of the just and unjust; "obey fully in all things or you shall be cursed." The son and servant would be all one, and the law would still command over the children with as much terror as over the bond-slave.

There is no difference in the world in our adversaries' doctrine. Both sorts are bound to obey perfectly or else certainly they shall not be saved. So the law of itself shall be as rigorous towards one as the other. But we know the Scriptures offer unto us more mercy, and that Christ has discharged us from this rigor of the law under which everyone who is outside of Him in the state of unbelief is held in bondage. As for the difference, they claim that the just obey willingly and the unjust unwillingly, and therefore the law compels these and not those, but this is nothing to the purpose. For it does not alter the nature of the law to say that it is obeyed with various affections. The law is the same as for its command and authority; howsoever it is obeyed, willingly or unwillingly, does not matter. The law does not cease to be coercive because it is willingly obeyed, even as a slave does not cease to be under the coercive and compelling power of his master though he loves his master, and out of a willing mind is content to abide in servitude. Similarly Adam, though he obeyed the law willingly, yet was under the coercive power of it because he was tied to obeying it, or else he would certainly die the death for his transgression of it. Wherefore I conclude that the just are not freed from the law's direction, but from the law's compulsion, as it compels or enjoins them to absolute obedience in all things, and for default thereof threatens the unavoidable curse of God's eternal wrath.

Lastly, for further proof of this point, we have those passages formerly cited: "We are not under the law, but under grace" (Romans 6:14). "If we be led by the Spirit, we are not under the law" (Galatians 5:18). "Now the lord is the Spirit, and where the Spirit of the Lord is, there is liberty" (2 Corinthians 3:17). "Christ hath redeemed us from the curse of the law, being made a curse for us" (Galatians 3:13). All of these, with many other passages (such as Romans 8:1–2), establish this orthodox doctrine that believers have obtained freedom by Christ from the rigor of the moral law, and are not any longer bound in conscience to the perfect fulfilling thereof upon the assured peril that if they do not keep it they shall not be saved.

We might stand longer upon each testimony, but let that which we have said suffice for the vindication of our conscience from that torture and bondage wherewith these popish doctors would ensnare us. The knowledge of our liberty is not to give us occasion of security or licentiousness, as these men calumniate, but to restore peace and spiritual rest unto our souls, knowing that we are now delivered from the necessity of obeying or of perishing, which, before we were in Christ, laid more heavily upon our souls than a mountain of lead. So, being freed from this bondage, we may serve Him who has freed us, thankfully and cheerfully obeying Him in all duty, by whom we have obtained this glorious privilege. Whereas perfect obedience was sometimes strictly exacted of us, now our sincere, though imperfect, endeavors shall be mercifully accepted from our hands.

SECTION VI

Chapter 15

The reconciliation of that seeming opposition between St. Paul and St. James in this point of justification

So much for this argument, and for the first branch of man's righteousness whereby, if it were possible, he should be justified, that is, his obedience to the law of God. By this means, we have shown, no flesh shall be justified in God's sight. We are to proceed unto the next branch thereof, man's satisfaction for his transgression of the law. Here we must also prove that a sinner cannot be acquitted before God's judgment seat by pleading any satisfaction that he himself can make for his offenses.

But in passing on to that point, we are to give you warning of that stumbling stone which St. James (as it may seem) has laid in our way, lest any should dash his faith upon it and fall, as our adversaries have done, into that error of justification by works. That blessed apostle, in the second chapter of his epistle, seems not only to give occasion to, but directly to teach this doctrine of justification by works. For in verse 21 and following, he expressly says that Abraham was justified by works when he offered his son Isaac upon the altar, and also that Rahab was in like manner justified by works when she entertained the spies.

Whence also he sets down a general conclusion that a man is justified by works, and not by faith alone (James 2:24).

Now at first glance, nothing can be spoken more contrary to St. Paul's doctrine in Romans and elsewhere. For speaking of the same example of Abraham, he says (exactly to the contrary) that Abraham was *not* justified by works, for then he might have boasted (Romans 4:2). And treating generally of man's justification by faith, after a strong dispute he draws forth the conclusion that a man is justified by faith without the works of the law (Romans 3:28). This conclusion appears contradictory to that of St. James. This harsh discord between these apostles appears to some as impossible to resolve by any qualification; knowing that the Holy Ghost never forgets Himself, some have concluded that if the Spirit of truth spoke by St. Paul, it was doubtless the spirit of error that spoke by the author of this epistle of James. For this cause, most likely, the epistle of James was doubted in ancient times, as Eusebius and Jerome witness, but yet then also publicly allowed in many churches, and ever since received in all.

Out of this, for the same cause, Luther and some of his followers since him would again throw it forth, accounting the author of it to have built no gold or silver, but straw and stubble upon the foundation. Erasmus assents to Luther. And Musculus agrees with them both; in his commentaries upon the fourth chapter of Romans he states simply that he does not see how James and Paul can be reconciled. Therefore he turns out St. James as the wrangler, supposing that this James was one of the disciples of James the Apostle, the brother of Christ, who, under pretense of his master's name and authority, continually snarled at the Apostle Paul and opposed his doctrine.

Reconciling Paul and James

Nevertheless his epistle got credit in later times when error by degrees prevailed against the truth.

But this medicine is worse than the disease, and is rather violence than skill thus to cut the knot where it cannot be readily untied. A safer and milder course may be held, and some means found out for the resolving of this grand difference, without robbing the Church of so much precious treasure of divine knowledge as is stored up in this epistle. Wherefore both they of the Romish and we of the Reformed Churches, admitting this epistle as canonical, do each search after a fit reconciliation between the apostles. But they and we are irreconcilable in our various reconciliations of them. They reconcile them by distinguishing justification and works.

Justification, they say, is of two sorts. The first is when an unjust man is made just and holy by the infusion of grace or the habit of charity. The second is when a just man is made more just by the augmentation of the habit of grace first given unto him.

Again they divide works into two sorts. Some go before faith, being performed by the mere strength of nature and free will, without the help of grace, and these works are not meritorious. Some follow faith, being performed by the aid and assistance of grace given unto man, and these works are meritorious.

These distinctions prepared, the work is now ready for the soldering which they finish, artificially gluing together the propositions of the two apostles in this way. St. Paul says that Abraham and all men are justified by faith without works. This, they say, is to be understood of the first justification, and of works done before faith without grace by the strength of nature. So that the meaning of Paul's proposition is that neither Abraham nor any other can deserve the grace of sanctification whereby, from being unjust and unholy, they are made just and holy by any works done by them when they are naturally men destitute of grace, but only after they have faith in Christ Jesus. In other words, no man merits grace to make him a good man rather than a bad one by anything he does before he believes in Christ, but by believing he obtains this grace. On the other hand, James says that Abraham and all others are justified by works, not by faith only. This, say the Romanists, is meant of the second justification and of such works as are done after faith by the aid of grace. So the meaning of the proposition shall be that Abraham and other men, being once made good and just, deserve to be made better and more just by such good works as they perform through the help of grace given unto them, and not by faith only. Being once sanctified, they deserve the increase of sanctification through that merit of their faith and good works out of faith and charity.

Do you not think this difference between these apostles to be finely bridged? But they cannot walk together as friends, according to this mediation of the scholastics. Rather, the Jesuits are so far from reconciling them that they have abused them both and set them farther asunder, making them speak what they never meant. Neither in Paul nor in James is there any ground at all whereon to raise such an interpretation of their words. And therefore we respect this reconciliation as the shifting quirk of a schoolman's brain who has no footing at all in the text. This we do upon these reasons:

1. That distinction of justification (that is, actually, of sanctification) into the first giving of it and the later increase of it, howsoever tolerable in other matters, is utterly to no purpose as it is applied unto the doctrine of these

apostles. When they speak of the justification of a sinner in God's sight, they understand thereby the remission of sins through the imputation of Christ's righteousness, and not the infusion or increase of inherent sanctity in the soul of man. This confusion of justification with sanctification is a prime error of our adversaries in this article, as has been shown in clarifying the meaning of the word "justification," and shall be shown at greater length when we discuss the form of our justification.

2. That distinction of justification taken in their own sense is falsely applied to St. James as if he spoke of the second justification, and to St. Paul as if he spoke of the first. For, first, Bellarmine himself points out that St. James in the example of Rahab speaks of the first justification because (as he says) she was then at first made a believer from an infidel, a righteous woman from a harlot. And again Paul speaks of the second justification in the example of Abraham, which is cited by both the apostles.

Here is then a confusion instead of a distinction. Paul speaks of the first, James speaks of the second, and yet both speak of both justifications. Again, when they say that James speaks of the second justification whereby a just man becomes more just, it is a groundless imagination, forasmuch as it would be to no purpose; for the Apostle James to treat of the second justification whereby men grow better, when those hypocrites with whom he had to do had erred from their first justification whereby they were not as yet made good, as the learned [Arthur] Jackson observes. Nay, there is not in St. James's entire dispute any syllable that may give any just suspicion that by justification he means the increase of inherent justice. Bellarmine catches at the clause "by works faith was made perfect" (James 2:22), which is, in the Jesuit's construction, Abraham's inherent justice begun by faith, receiving increase and perfection by his works. But this is only the Jesuit's frenzy. Abraham's faith and his righteousness, whereof his faith is but a part, were not made perfect, but were *declared* to be perfect—by the perfect work which it brought forth, as even Lorinus, another of that sect, expounds it orthodoxly.

3. That distinction between works done before faith without grace, and after faith by grace, is to as little purpose as the former distinction in this matter of our justification. Heretofore we have touched upon that distinction and shown the vanity thereof in limiting St. Paul to works done without grace, when he simply excludes all works from our justification. And James, though he requires works of grace to be joined with that faith which must justify us, yet does not gives them that place and office in our justification from which Paul excludes them, and wherein our adversaries would establish them, as shall appear shortly.

Leaving, then, this sophistic reconcilement coined by our adversaries, I come to those reconciliations which are made by our divines, wherein we shall have better satisfaction upon better grounds. There are two ways whereby our men reconcile this seeming difference.

The first way is by distinguishing the word "justification," which may be taken either for the absolution of a sinner in God's judgment or for the declaration of a man's righteousness before men. This distinction is certain, and has its ground in Scripture, which uses the word "justify" in both ways, for the acquitting of us in God's sight and for the manifestation of our innocence before man against accusation or suspicion of fault. They apply this distinction to reconcile the two apostles thus: Paul

Reconciling Paul and James

speaks of justification in the forum of God; James speaks of justification in the forum of man. A man is justified by faith without works, says Paul; that is, in God's sight a man obtains remission of sins and is reputed to be just only for his faith in Christ, not for his works' sake. A man is justified by works and not by faith only, says James; that is, in man's sight we are declared to be just by our good works and not by our faith only, which with other inward and invisible graces is made visible unto man only in the good works which they see us perform. That this application is not unfit to reconcile this difference may be shown by the following analysis.

First, as for Paul, it is agreed on all sides that he speaks of man's justification in God's sight (Romans 3:20).

Second, as for James, we are to show that with just probability he may be understood as referring to the declaration of our justification and righteousness before men. For proof thereof, the text affords us these reasons.

"Show me thy faith without thy works, and I will show thee my faith by my works" (James 2:18). Here the true Christian, speaking to the hypocritical boaster of his faith, requires of him a declaration of his faith and justification thereby by a real proof, not a verbal profession, promising for his part to manifest and prove the truth of his own faith by his good works. Whence it appears that, before man, none can justify the soundness of his faith but by his works thence proceeding.

Abraham is said to be justified "when he offered up his son Isaac upon the altar" (James 2:21). Now it is manifest that Abraham was justified in God's sight long before, even 25 years earlier (Genesis 15:6). Therefore, by that admirable work of his in offering his son he was declared before all the world to be a just man and a true believer. And for this purpose God tempted Abraham in that trial of his faith, that thereby all believers might behold a rare pattern of a lively and justifying faith, and see that Abraham was not without good cause called "the father of the faithful."

It is said that Abraham's faith "wrought with his works, and by works was his faith made perfect" (James 2:22). Even in the judgment of popish expositors, such as Lorinus, this is to be understood of the manifestation of Abraham's faith by his works. His faith directed his works; his works manifested the power and perfection of his faith.

It is not, then, without good probability of reason that Calvin and other expositors on our side have given this solution to the problem. Bellarmine labors against it, and would fain prove that justification cannot be taken here as referring to a declaration of righteousness. But his argument cannot much trouble any intelligent reader, and therefore I spare to trouble you with his sophistry.

This now is the first way of reconciling these two passages. Nevertheless, although this approach may be defended against anything that our adversaries object to the contrary, yet many very learned divines choose rather to tread in another path, and more nearly to press the apostles' steps, whom also in this point I willingly follow.

The second way, then, of reconciling these passages is by distinguishing the word "faith," which is taken in a double sense. It is first taken for that faith which is true and living (faith which works through love), and is fruitful in all manner of obedience. Second, it is taken for that faith which is false and dead, being only a bare acknowledgment of the truth of all articles of religion accompanied with an outward formality of profession, but yet destitute of sincere obedience.

This distinction of this word "faith" is certain by the Scriptures, as has heretofore been shown in our discussions of that grace. Our men now apply it thus: When Paul affirms that we are justified by faith only, he speaks of that faith which is true and living, working by charity. When James denies that a man is justified by faith only, he disputes against that faith which is false and dead, without power to bring forth any good works. So that the apostles speak no contradiction, because Paul teaches that we are justified by a true faith and James affirms that we are not justified by a false faith.

Again, Paul says we are not justified by works; James says we are justified by works. Neither is there any contradiction at all here. For James understands by "works" a working faith, in opposition to the idle and dead faith before spoken of, by a metonymy of the effect. Whence it is plain that these two propositions, that we are *not* justified by works (which is Paul's) and that we *are* justified by a working faith (which is James's), sweetly consort together. Paul severs works from our justification, but not from our faith. James joins works to our faith, but not to our justification.

Let me make this a little plainer by a similitude or two. There is a great difference between these two sayings: A man lives by a reasonable soul, and a man lives by reason. The former is true, and shows us what qualities and power are essential unto that soul whereby a man lives. But the latter is false, because we do not live by the quality or power of reason, though we live by that soul which has that quality necessarily belonging to it, without which it is no human soul. So also in these propositions: The shoot lives through its authoring life breath; the shoot lives through its growth. Any puny mind can tell that the former is true and the other false. For, although in the vegetative soul whereby plants live, there are necessarily required for its existence those three faculties of nourishment, growth, and procreation, yet it is not the faculty of growing that gives life unto plants, for they live when they are not growing.

In like manner, these two propositions—that we are justified by a working faith and that we are justified by works—differ greatly. The first is true and shows us what qualities are necessarily required unto the existence of that faith, whereby the just shall live, namely that beside the power of believing in the promise there is also a habitual proneness and resolution unto the doing of all good works joined with it. But the later proposition is false. For although true faith is equally as apt to work in bringing forth universal obedience to God's will as it is apt to believe and trust perfectly in God's promises, yet nevertheless we are not justified by it as it brings forth good works, but as it embraces the promises of the gospel.

Now, then, James affirms that which is true, that we are justified by a working faith, and Paul denies that which is false, that we are justified by works.

Chapter 16

The confirmation of the orthodox reconciliation of St. Paul and St. James by a logical analysis of James 2

This reconciliation is the fairest, and has the most certain grounds in the text. It will, I doubt not, appear so unto you when it shall be cleared from these cavils that can be made against it. There are but two things in it that may cause our adversaries to quarrel. The first is regarding the word "faith." We say that James speaks of a false and counterfeit faith. They say he speaks of that which is true, though dead without works. This is one point.

The second is concerning the interpretation of the word "works" used by James when he says that we are justified by works. This we interpret by a metonymy of the effect for the cause: We are justified by a working faith, by that faith which is apt to declare and show itself in all good works. This interpretation may perhaps prove distasteful to their nicer palates who are very ready, when it fits their mood, to grate sorely upon the bare words and letter of a text. These cavils removed, this reconciliation will appear to be sure and good.

To accomplish this, I suppose nothing will be more commodious than to present unto you a brief resolution of the whole dispute of James regarding faith, that by a plain and true exposition thereof we may more easily discover the cavils and sophistic forgeries wherewith our adversaries have pestered this place of Scripture. The disputation is found in James 2:14–26.

The scope and sum here is a sharp reprehension of the hypocritical faith of "vain men," as they are called in verse 20, who in the apostle's time under pretense of religion thought they might live as they wished. There were two extremes unto which these Jews to whom the apostle writes were misled by false teachers and their own corruptions. The first was that, notwithstanding faith in Christ, they were bound to fulfill the whole law of Moses, against which Paul disputed in his epistle to the Galatians who also were infected with that leaven. The other was that faith in Christ was sufficient without any regard to obedience to the law; if people believed the gospel, acknowledging the articles of religion as true, and made an outward profession, all would be well, even if in the meantime sanctity and sincere obedience were quite neglected. The former error brought them into bondage; this one made them licentious. It is certainly a pleasing heresy, of which there were and will always be plenty of followers who content themselves to have a form of godliness, but deny the power thereof. Against such hypocrites and vain boasters of false faith and false religion, St. James disputes in this passage, showing plainly that such men leaned on a staff of reed, deceiving themselves with a counterfeit and shadow of true Christian faith instead of the substance.

The reproof with the main reason is expressed by way of interrogation in verse 14: "What doth it profit, my brethren, though a man say he hath faith, and have not works?" Many then did, and always will, say that they have faith, boasting falsely of that which they do not have in truth, that is, obedience to God's will whereby to prove that faith they boast of. "Can that faith save him?" Is that faith without works a saving faith that will bring a man to

A Logical Analysis of James 2

heaven?

These sharp interrogations must be resolved into their strong negations. And so we have these two propositions, the one containing the main theme of the apostle's dispute, the other a general reason for it. The first is that faith without obedience is unprofitable. The second, proving the first, is that faith without obedience will not save a man.

The whole argument is that faith which will not save a man is unprofitable, of no use. But the faith which is without obedience will not save. Ergo, faith without obedience is unprofitable.

The major premise of this argument will easily be granted, that it is an unprofitable faith which will not bring a man to life and happiness. But how does St. James prove the minor premise, that a faith without works will not do that?

Though it scarcely needs any proof, yet because hypocrisy is ever armed with sophistry, in order to be plainer, the apostle proves it by this manner of argumentation: That faith which saves a man is a true faith. But a faith without works is not a true faith. Ergo, a faith without works will not save a man.

The major premise is evident to all who have reason. The minor premise St. James proves by various arguments.

ARGUMENT 1. The first is contained in verses 15 to 17, and it is drawn from comparison with another similar virtue, namely charity toward the poor. The argument is thus: If charity towards the poor, professed inwardly but without works, is counterfeit, then faith in God, professed in like manner without obedience, is also counterfeit and not true. But charity towards the poor in words professed without deeds is a counterfeit charity. Ergo, faith in God without obedience is a counterfeit and false faith.

The truth of the major proposition is evident from the similitude there is between all virtues and graces. There is no virtue but men may counterfeit and falsely arrogate it to themselves, as they may boast of a false faith (as Solomon and experience speak of) a false liberality, false valor, false prudence. Now there is but one way to discover this type of counterfeiting, and that is to go from word to works, from presumptions and boastings to action. This method all count most certain, nor will any man believe words against works, or be persuaded by fair speeches that the habits of the virtues and graces are truly seated in the mind of one whose tongue tells us they are so, but whose doings confute his sayings. Wherefore the apostle, in his comparison, proceeds on an undeniable ground.

We now return to the minor premise, that the charity which is rich in good words and poor in alms-deeds is not true but counterfeit pity. The apostle shows this by an ordinary instance. If a brother or sister is naked or destitute of daily food (that is, if a believing Christian needs food and raiment or other necessities), and one of you says unto them, "Depart in peace and be ye warmed and filled"; if he gives him kind words, "Alas, poor soul, I pity you and wish you well. I would I had something to give you. Go in God's name where you may be relieved," and so lets him pass with a few pitiful compliments, but not offering them those things which are needful for the body—what does it profit? Is the poor man's back ever the warmer, or his belly the fuller, with a few windy compliments? Can such a man persuade anyone that he has a heart of mercy and compassion towards the needy when they find such cold entertainment at his gates? It is manifest that this is but a mere mockery, and that such pitiful words do not come not from a heart that is truly merciful.

The apostle now applies this lesson regarding charity unto faith: "Even so faith, if it have not works is dead, being alone" (James 2:17). As that charity, so also that faith which men profess without obedience is false and feigned, and therefore unprofitable to save a man. It is dead. How must this be understood? Faith is a quality of the soul, and qualities are said to be dead when they are extinguished. It is as if we should say, "Such a man's charity is dead." It is because he has lost it; that which was in him is abolished.

But this is not the meaning, for then when James says that faith is dead, being alone, his meaning would be that faith severed from works is not faith at all, but quite extinguished. Now this is not so, for there is a faith severed from works in hypocrites, heretics, reprobates, and devils. This faith is a general assent to all divine truths, and this faith in them has a true existence but no saving use. Wherefore it is called a "dead faith" in regard to the effect, because there is nothing in it to bring them in whom it exists to life and salvation, as a true and living faith has.

Here our adversaries have much strange contemplation, telling us that faith without works, though it is a dead faith, it is yet a true faith, even as an instrument is a true instrument though it is not used. So that, in their philosophy, it is one and the same true faith which is dead without and living with works, even as it is one and the same body which lives with the soul and is dead without it, or as water is the same whether it stands still in a cistern, or runs into a river. Whence they proceed to discourse that charity is a form of faith, and conclude that it is not the inward and essential form of it, as the soul is the form of a man (for works are not essential to faith), nor the accidental form, as whiteness is of paper, because faith according to their schools is in the understanding and charity in the will. Rather, charity is the external form of it, because it gives to faith a merit and worthiness to deserve heaven.

These fond speculations on the form and merit of faith I pass by now, having touched upon them heretofore. As for their claim that a living faith and a dead faith are one and the same true faith, that is utterly false; they differ as much as light and darkness. First, they differ in their subject: A dead faith is in reprobate men and devils, a living faith only in the elect. Second, they differ in their object: A dead faith assents to divine revelations as barely true or good only in general; living faith assents to them as truer and better in themselves than anything that can be set against them. Third, in their nature: A dead faith is no sanctifying grace, but a common gift of creation (as found even in the devil), and of ordinary illumination, as in reprobate men; a living faith is a sanctifying grace, a part of inherent holiness wrought in the heart by the special power of the Holy Ghost. All this has been heretofore shown in handling the nature of faith.

Unto those arguments, or sophisms rather, which Bellarmine brings to prove that James speaks of a true divine, infused, catholic, Christian faith, though it is dead faith, I answer briefly. We grant a dead faith to be a true faith, but only in its kind. It has a true being in men and devils in whom it exists, and it is directed toward true objects. But it is not that true faith which is catholic, Christian, and saving. This is of another kind, and, in comparison to this one, that other is but a mere shadow and counterfeit resemblance of true faith. Wherefore, when those hypocrites accounted themselves to have that faith which is truly Christian and saving, James showed them that their faith which was alone, devoid of obedience, was nothing but a faith of another kind, a dead faith, having only a false show of a true and living faith.

ARGUMENT 2. The second argument is contained in verse 18, being drawn from an impossibility. The argument stands thus: that faith which is truly Christian may be shown and proven so to be. But a faith without works cannot be demonstrated to be a true faith. Ergo, a faith without works is no true faith.

The major premise is passed over as most evident of itself, because there any moral virtue or grace of the Holy Ghost truly planted in the heart may be known by some external actions which it is apt to bring forth, even as life is known by breathing or beating of the pulse. The truth of an invisible grace has its demonstration in visible works.

As for for the minor premise, James proves that faith without obedience cannot appear by any proof to be true faith. He does this in a dialogue between a true believer and a hypocrite. "A man may say, 'Thou hast faith, and I have works'; show me thy faith without works, and I will show thee my faith by my works." That is, you say you have a true faith, though you have no works. I say I have true faith because I have works. We come now to the trial, and let it appear who speaks truly, you or I. If you speak truly, prove your faith by something or other to be true. Show me your faith without your works. If you have no works whereby to show your faith, make it then appear by something else; but that is impossible. Where works are wanting, there is no other demonstration whereby to justify the truth of faith. And therefore you are driven to confess that you vainly boast of that which you do not have.

"But on the other side," says the true believer, "I can

make good that which I say, proving that my faith is true by my works. I will show you my faith by my works. My sincere obedience is a real demonstration that my belief is no verbal ostentation and vain bragging."

This proof of St. James is very convincing and grips the conscience of hypocrites, smiting them with shame and confusion when they come to this trial, and so causing their false and fraudulent hearts to be laid open.

But here it will be asked what works demonstrate the truth of faith, and also how they prove it.

We answer that works are of two sorts: ordinarily, such works of sanctity and obedience as are required as part of a holy conduct; extraordinarily, miracles. We say that James refers to the former, and those only. Our adversaries claim that he means both, but erroneously, forasmuch as St. James speaks not of the doctrine of faith, but of the grace of faith. The grace of faith requires good works of piety and charity as perpetually necessary to confirm its truth. So the doctrine of faith does not always require miraculous works for the confirmation of its divinity, but only at the first publication thereof. Wherefore Lorinus is very ridiculous when he tells us that they may justly demand of us heretics (for so they declare us) miracles for the confirmation of our new and false doctrine.

Indeed, were it new and false, their request would not be unreasonable that we should make our doctrine credible by doing miracles. But surely the Jesuit judges our doctrine by his own. Did he not suspect our doctrine to be a new error, there would be no reason to require miracles for confirmation of an old truth. As for ourselves, we do not seek the aid of a lying wonder to uphold a true doctrine, nor do we count it any disgrace at all to our religion that we cannot by our faith so much as cure a lame horse (as the Jesuit, citing Erasmus, scoffs at us).

Now, surely, if such a beast as Bellarmine's devout mare needs help to set her on all fours, we cannot be yet so well persuaded of that virtue of Romish faith as to think that a friar will do more good than a blacksmith. But where the Jesuit goes on to require of us the other sort of good works (of piety and charity) for the demonstration of our faith, he has reason to do so, though not so much as he imagines when he charges us with neglect of good works and unbridled licentiousness. Would to God that we could clear our practice from such neglect as well as we can our doctrine from recommending it. But if we make a comparison, we know no reason why we should run behind the door as more ashamed of our practices than they may justly be of theirs—in which case we bid him among them who is without sin to cast the first stone at us.

To proceed, given that works of obedience are the proofs of a true faith, it must be considered in what sort they prove it. For may not good works be counterfeited as well as faith?

I answer that in this trial, the judgment of verity and infallibility belongs unto God, who alone knows the heart and conscience, being able to discern every secret working of the soul, and so to judge exactly whether or not all outward appearances come from inward sincerity. But as for the judgment of charity that belongs to us, if we behold in any man the works of obedience to God's will, of such a man we are to judge that he has true faith, though yet herein we must, as far as human frailty will give leave, judge also not according to appearance, but with righteous judgments. Men's practices must be examined. If hypocrisy betrays itself (as it is hard for a counterfeit not to betray himself at some time or another if he is duly observed), there charity must not be blind. It must see and censure it. It is not a charitable, but a perverse judgment to call evil good; nor is it any offense to call that a barren or bad tree that bears either no fruit at all or none but bad. And so much for this second argument of the Apostle, that the faith of these hypocrites is vain because when it comes to the proof it cannot be justified to be sound and good.

ARGUMENT 3. The third argument, contained in verse 19, from the example of the devils themselves, in whom there is a faith without works as well as in hypocrites. And therefore it is in neither of them a true faith. The argument is brought in to confute a cavil which the hypocrite might make against the former reason. "True," he might say, "I cannot show my faith by my works, yet for all that I have a true faith. And why? Because I believe the articles of religion, that there is one God," with the rest. Hereto the apostle replies that such a belief is not a true Christian faith, because it is to be found even in the devils.

The argument runs thus: that faith which is in the devils is no true Christian faith. But a bare assent to the articles of religion without obedience is in the devils. Ergo, a bare assent without obedience is no true Christian faith.

The major premise of this argument will easily be granted, that the devils do not have that true faith which is required of a Christian man for his salvation. The minor premise is also evident, that the devils believe the articles of Christian religion. St. James gives one example, namely the article of the Godhead, whereto the devils assent as well as hypocritical men. "Thou believest that there is one God," says the true believer to the hypocrite, who pleads that he believes the articles of faith, "thou doest well. It is a laudable and good thing to acknowledge the truth of religion. But withal, you must know that the devils deserve as much commendation for this belief as you do. The devils also believe this; they even confess the truth of that and other articles of religion. An evident proof of this is that they tremble at the power, wrath, and justice of God, and the remembrance of the last judgment, which, did they not believe, they would not fear."

But now they expect it with horror, because they know it will come upon them. Whence it is plain that the faith of hypocrites and devils is all one, neither better than the other, both unfruitful to bring forth obedience, both unprofitable to bring one unto salvation, and therefore neither of them is that true faith which is Christian and saving. This argument of the apostle pinches our adversaries sorely who stiffly maintain that James speaks of a true, though of a dead, faith. For they cannot dare to say that there is a true faith in the devils and damned spirits. But James has concluded that they have that dead faith of which hypocrites boast. What then? A dead faith is no true faith, as our adversaries affirm it is. Wherefore, to help themselves, they deny that it is one and the same dead faith which is in hypocrites and evil spirits. Indeed, in regard to the object, they grant that the faith of devils is as true and catholic as that of wicked men, because they both believe the same things. And also in regard to the effects they grant their faith to be alike, because both are unfruitful; but not from the part of the subject—here they say there is much difference. The faith of devils is of one sort, and the faith of hypocrites of another.

But here they become a little too bold with the blessed apostle, overturning the force of his argument to uphold their own fancy. The apostle proves against hypocrites that their idle faith without obedience is not true saving faith.

Why? Because the devils' idle faith, destitute of obedience, is no true saving faith. But now, is the faith of devils and hypocrites of the same kind and nature? Yes or no? No, they are not. They are of a different nature, say the adversaries. Let it be then considered what force there is in the apostle's argument: faith without works in devils saves them not; therefore faith without works in wicked men saves them not. Might not one, prompted by a Jesuit, reply to the apostle, "Nay, by your leave, your argument is flawed because you do not define your terms properly. Faith in the devils is of one kind, and faith in hypocrites is of another; therefore though faith without works cannot save devils, yet faith without works may save men"? Thus would the apostle's argument be laid in the dust if these men's opinions may stand as good. But would you know what distinction these men make between the faith of devils and of wicked men, which St. James takes to be the same? It is that the faith of evil men is free while the faith of devils is compelled and extorted from them by a kind of force. So Bellarmine says, "The faith of evil men is free for the service of Christ by the undoubtedly pious will captivating the understanding; the faith of the demons is indeed compelled and extracted from the evidence of things itself. The same thing James arrived at, saying, 'The demons believe, and they tremble.' For we do not believe trembling, that is, unwillingly and under compulsion, but freely and joyfully."

Wicked men believe freely and willingly. Why? Because their pious and godly will makes captive their understanding to the obedience of Christ, so causing it to assent unto the truth. The devils believe upon compulsion, being forced to it by the evidence of the things themselves, which St. James intimates. They believe and tremble; that is, they believe against their wills. Is not this a shameless Jesuit, who will say anything to patch up a broken cause? For are these not absurd contradictions, to say that wicked men have godly wills, that by a pious motion of the will their understanding is made captive to the obedience of Christ, and yet they are hypocrites and wicked men still? No man can relish such assertions who knows how averse and froward the will of men is to embrace anything from God till such time as it is regenerated by sanctifying grace.

It is therefore contrary to reason to affirm that wicked men believe willingly, and it is against experience which shows that ungodly men are utterly as unwilling to believe any truth that goes against them in any way whatsoever as a bear is to be brought to the stake. Indeed, in matters that pleasure them, or in such as are of an indifferent nature, neither feeding nor crossing their corruptions, they will be apt to believe, though not out of a pious affection, as the Jesuit dreams, but out of self-love and other selfish considerations. But in any point of religion that in any way grates upon their wicked affections, all the persuasion and instruction in the world cannot work them in to a belief of it till the conscience (in spite of their hearts) is convicted by some notable evidence of the truth.

Now what else can be said of the devils, who will as willingly believe what serves them (if anything did) or does not go against them as any wicked man does? And they are as unwilling to believe anything what makes against them as any wicked man is. Nor would they believe it did not the clearness of divine revelations convince them of the certain truth thereof. So there is no difference at all, in that they both believe unwillingly; as devils, so wicked men believe with trembling. The devils indeed believe with greater horror, as their belief and knowledge are always more distinct than man's. But yet men believe with horror too, when their consciences are awakened by fits to behold the woes that are coming upon them.

Along with this distinction made by Bellarmine and others we must consider two more: first, that the faith of devils is natural while that of wicked men is supernatural and infused; that the faith of devils is dishonest while the faith of wicked men is an honest faith. Concerning the first difference, we grant indeed that the faith of the devils is not supernatural, except in regard to the object. The faculties which they received in their creation are not so far corrupted in them but that they are able to assent unto and apprehend divine revelations without further help than of their own natural abilities.

Man, in his fall, sustained greater loss in the spiritual powers of his soul and therefore stands in need of help. This help is afforded even unto the ungodly; but this is by ordinary illumination, not by special infusion of any sanctifying grace. They are enlightened above the ordinary pitch of natural blindness, but not above that whereto a mere natural understanding may be advanced. Yea, were man's understanding raised up to that perfection which is in devils, this would be more than nature, yet still less than grace. This common gift of illumination bestowed on wicked men, but not on devils, is no proof that their faith is of a different kind.

As for the second difference, we are not so far studied in morality as to conceive wherein the dishonesty of the devil's faith and the honesty of the hypocrite's faith lie. To ordinary understanding it seems every way as honest and commendable a matter for a wicked fiend as for a wicked man to believe what God reveals unto him. If not, we must ask to be further informed by these Jesuits, men who are better read in that part of ethics, whether it is diabolical or hypocritical.

ARGUMENT 4. The fourth argument is contained in verses 20–25, before which the apostle repeats his main conclusion that faith without obedience is a false and dead faith. "But will thou know, O vain man (or hypocrite), that faith without works is dead?" (James 2:20).

To convince him further, he proceeds to a new argument to prove unto him that the faith which will not justify a man is a false and dead faith. But the faith which is without works will not justify a man. Ergo, it is a dead and a false faith.

The major premise the apostle omits, as most evident of itself. The minor premise he proves by induction from two examples. If Abraham and Rahab were justified by a working faith, then that faith which is without works will not justify. But Abraham and Rahab were justified by a working faith. Ergo, faith without works will not justify a man.

The basis for the consequence is manifest, because, as Abraham and Rahab are justified, so must all others be justified. The means of justification and life were ever one and the same for all men. This also the apostle intimates in that clause of verse 21, "Was not our father Abraham," implying that, as the father, so also the children. The whole stock and generation of the faithful were and are still justified by one uniform means. The two instances the apostle urges are that of Abraham (verses 21–23) and that of Rahab (verse 25). The conclusion which issues equally from them both he places in the midst, after the presentation of Abraham's example (verse 24). I shall go over them as they lie in the text.

In the example of Abraham, the apostle sets down the

proposition that Abraham was justified by a working faith (James 2:21). For this interrogative, "Was not our father Abraham justified by works?" must be resolved into an affirmative: "Abraham our father was justified by works, that is, a working faith." This proposition the apostle confirms by its parts: first, showing that Abraham's faith was an operative faith, declared and approved by his works; second, proving that by such a working faith Abraham was justified in God's sight. To show that the faith of Abraham was operative, full of life and power to bring forth obedience unto God, the apostle alleges one instance: Abraham's singular work of obedience unto God's command when he offered up his son Isaac upon the altar. Many other works were performed by Abraham, abundantly justifying the truth of his faith; but the apostle chooses this one above all others as that work which was purposely enjoined him by God as a trial of his faith. In this action, Abraham, mightily overcoming all of those strong temptations to disobedience and infidelity, made it appear that his faith was not an idle, dead, and empty speculation, but an active and working grace.

Wherefore the apostle adds in verse 22, "Seest thou how faith wrought with his works, and by works was faith made perfect?" That is, as in other works of that holy patriarch, so especially in that sacrificing of his son all who can see may plainly behold the strength and life of his faith. Faith is wrought with his works. That is, his faith directed and supported him in the doing of that work, as the writer of Hebrews expounds it. By faith Abraham offered up Isaac (Hebrews 11:17). That work would not have been done if faith had not wrought it. In every circumstance thereof faith did all in all, from the beginning of the work to the end. This interpretation is most simple and generally received. Faith wrought with—that is, in or by—his works unto the performance whereof the force of faith was in special manner assisting. Pareus reads it thus: "Faith being with his works wrought what? His justification." But his construction seems somewhat hard, and not necessary for this place. The other interpretation is much plainer, showing us by or with what virtue Abraham's works were wrought, that is, by the virtue of his faith, which in a most powerful manner incited and enabled him to obey.

The apostle goes on, "and by works was made perfect," that is, declared to be perfect. For works did not perfect Abraham's faith essentially, inasmuch as long before this time it was perfect, as is plain in that Abraham was justified by it 25 years before the oblation of his son Isaac and also, by the strength of his faith, had done many excellent works and obtained great blessings at the hand of God. So that the offering up of Isaac was not the cause, but a fruit of the perfection of Abraham's faith; the great difficulty of the work showed the singular perfection of that grace which was able so to encounter and conquer it. The goodness of the fruit does not work, but declares the goodness that is in the tree. The quality of the fruit always depends upon the nature of the tree, but the contrary is not true. Thus then the first part of the proposition is plainly proved by the apostle: Abraham's faith was a lively and working faith, declaring and approving its own truth by the works of his obedience.

The next part, namely that Abraham was justified in God's sight by such a working faith, he proves, first, by a testimony of Scripture, and second, by an effect or consequence thereof. Both are expressed in verse 23, the first in these words: "And the Scripture was fulfilled which sayeth,

'Abraham believed God, and it was imputed unto him for righteousness.' " The application of this testimony is very heedfully to be observed because it serves excellently to clarify the apostle's meaning when he says we are justified by works. "And the Scripture was fulfilled," says James. When? At the time when Isaac was offered. But was it not fulfilled before that time? Yes, many years before, when the promise of the blessed seed was made unto him, as appears in Genesis 15:6, from whence this testimony is taken.

How was it then fulfilled at the oblation of Isaac? In this way: the truth of that which was verified before was then again confirmed by a new and evident experiment. Well, this much is plain enough. But here now the difficulty is how this Scripture is applied unto the apostle's former dispute. In verse 21 he says that Abraham was justified by works when he offered Isaac. How does he prove that he was so justified? By this testimony: Because the Scripture was fulfilled at that time which says, "Abraham believed God."

Mark, then, the apostle's argument: When Abraham offered Isaac the Scripture was fulfilled which says, "Abraham was justified by faith." For that is the meaning of that Scripture. Therefore Abraham, when he offered Isaac, was justified by works.

At first sight this seems far-fetched, and not only so, but also quite contrary to the apostle's purpose, to prove that he was justified by works, because the Scripture says he was justified by faith. But upon due consideration the inference appears to be evident and the argument easy. The apostle and the Scripture have one and the same meaning: He was justified by faith, meaning, as all confess, a working faith fruitful in obedience. James affirms the

A Logical Analysis of James 2

very same thing, saying that he was justified by works, that is, metonymically, by a working faith.

And therefore the apostle rightly cites the Scripture in confirmation of his assertion. The Scripture witnesses that by faith he was justified; the apostle expounds what manner of faith it means, namely a faith with works or a working faith. So that the application of this testimony unto that time of the offering up of Isaac is most excellent, because then it appeared manifestly by what manner of faith it was that God had accounted him to be just in former times. Without the metonymy there does not appear to be any force in the application of this Scripture and the argument from thence. The Scripture witnesses that Abraham was justified by faith. Therefore it is true that he was justified by works—what sense is there in this argument unless we expound St. James as using the metonymy that "works" means a working faith?

And so the argument holds firm. Take it otherwise, as our adversaries would have it—or, to speak truly, according to the former interpretation of our divines—and it breeds an absurd construction either way. Abraham in offering Isaac was justified by works, that is (by the second meaning of justification), from being good he was made better. How is that proved? By Scripture, because the Scripture says that at that time he was justified by faith. That is (by the first meaning of justification), from being bad he became good. Is not this most apparent nonsense? Again, according to the interpretations of our divines, Abraham, at the offering up of Isaac, was justified by works, that is, they say, declared to be just before men. How is that proved? By Scripture, because the Scriptures say that at that time he was justified by faith, that is, accounted to be just in God's sight. In this kind of argument, I must confess, I do not apprehend how there is any tolerable logic.

Wherefore we expound St. James metonymically, putting the effect for the cause, works for a working faith, as the necessary connection of the text forces us to do. Nor is there any harshness at all, nor violent straining in this figure, when two things of necessary and near dependence one upon another (such as works and a working faith) are put one for another. Neither have our adversaries more cause to complain of us for this figurative interpretation of works than we have of them for their figurative interpretation of faith. For when we are said to be justified by faith, they understand it to mean by faith that is properly ordered and meritorious, not formal; that is, faith in itself is not our sanctification, nor yet the cause of it, but it merits the bestowing of it and disposes us to receive it.

Let reason judge now which is the harsher exposition. Theirs says that faith justifies, that is, faith is a disposition in us deserving that God should sanctify us by infusion of the habit of charity. Ours says that works justify, that is, the faith whereby we are acquitted in God's sight is a working faith. So much for this testimony of Scripture proving that Abraham was justified by a true and working faith.

In the next place, the apostle shows it by a visible effect or consequence that followed upon his justification, as expressed in the next words: "And he was called the friend of God." It is a high prerogative for God the Creator to reckon a poor, mortal man as his familiar friend. But so entire and true was the faith of Abraham, so upright was his heart, that God not only graciously accounted it to him for righteousness, but also, in token of that gracious acceptance, entered into a league with Abraham, taking him for his special friend and confederate in a league both offensive and defensive. God would be a friend to Abraham ("Thou shalt be a blessing"), a friend of Abraham's friends ("I will bless them that bless thee"), and an enemy of Abraham's enemies ("I will curse them that curse thee"). This league of friendship with Abraham before the offering up of Isaac was thereupon renewed by solemn protestation and oath, as we have it in Genesis 22:16–18.

Thus we have this first example of Abraham. From thence the apostle proceeds to a general conclusion in the next verse: "Ye see then how that by works a man is justified, and not by faith only" (James 2:24). That is, therefore it is evident that a man is justified by a working faith, not by faith without works. This metonymical interpretation is again confirmed by the inference of this conclusion from the former verse. The Scripture says that "Abraham believed God and it was imputed unto him for righteousness." Therefore, says James, "Ye see how a man is justified by works, and not by faith only."

A man might here say, "Nay, rather, we see the contrary, that a man is justified by faith only, and not by works. For in that passage of Scripture no mention at all is made of works." Wherefore, of necessity, since we must understand both passages in the same sense, the conclusion follows directly that every man is justified by an active faith, and not an idle one, because the Scripture witnesses that Abraham was justified by the like faith.

Our adversaries conclusion, then, from this passage (that faith and works are partners in justification, and that we are justified partly by faith and partly by works) is vain and illogical. For when the apostle says that a man is justified by works and not by faith alone, his meaning is not that works and faith are two coordinate causes, by their joint force working our justification, but the apostle utterly excludes faith only from justification and attributes it wholly unto works. For by "faith only" he means faith alone, that faith which is alone, solitary, by itself, without works (verse 17). And such a dead faith, whereof these hypocrites boasted, St. James excludes wholly from justifying a man. I say then that he is not justified by faith only, but that he is justified by works, that is, a working faith that is fruitful in obedience.

The apostle goes forward from the example of Abraham unto that of Rahab. "Likewise was not Rahab the harlot justified by works?" (James 2:25). That is, in the same manner as Abraham, so also Rahab was justified by a working faith. This appeared to be so by that which she did when she received the messengers, entertained the two spies who were sent to search the land, and lodged them in her house without revealing them. And when by accident they were made known, she hid them secretly upon the roof and afterwards sent them out another way, conveying them away secretly, not by the usual way, but by another one, that is, through the window, letting them down over the wall by a cord, as the story has it. In this dangerous enterprise, wherein this weak woman ventured her life in succoring the enemies of her king and country, it appears plainly that she had a strong and lively faith in the God of Israel, and that the confession which she made with her mouth to the spies, "The Lord your God, He is the God in heaven above, and in the earth beneath" (Joshua 2:11), proceeded from a truly believing heart, inasmuch as her words were made good by works that followed them.

Wherefore the apostle justly compares these two examples of Abraham offering his son and Rahab in the kind usage of the spies, because both those facts were singular trials of a lively faith which was able in those situations to overcome what was hardest to conquer, natural affection. In Abraham fatherly affection for the life of a dear and only son, and in Rahab the natural love for one's country and one's own life, all stooped and gave way when true faith commanded obedience.

Here again our adversaries trouble themselves and the text with needless speculations, telling us that now the apostle has altered his cliff and has gone from the second meaning of justification in Abraham's example to the first meaning of justification in this of Rahab. They say that Rahab was converted at this time of receiving the spies, being made a believer from an infidel, a good woman from a bad one. They say that she, by this good work, expiated her former sins and merited the grace and favor of God, notwithstanding that she committed a venial sin in handling the business, telling a downright lie, which, though she should not have done it, yet did not hinder the meritoriousness of the work. They add on other fond imaginations, perverting the simplicity of the truth.

But, first, they are not agreed among themselves whether the apostle in this place shifts from one justification to another. Bellarmine affirms it, and many others do too. But others deny it, as may be seen in Lorinus' exposition of James 2:21. And were they agreed upon it, I am sure that they would disagree with the apostle, who makes this second instance of the same nature with the former. In like manner, he says, was Rahab justified as Abraham was. Again, when they say Rahab became a true believer at that time of receiving the spies, not before, it is more than they can prove. By the circumstances of the story it appears plainly that she believed before they came, by the relation of the great works which God had done for His people and the promises that were made unto them that they should possess Rahab's country. This bred fear in others, but faith in her, by the secret working of the Holy Ghost (Joshua 2:9–11).

And certainly, had she not had faith before the spies came, who can think she would have given lodging to such dangerous persons? But she knew them to be the servants of the God of Israel in whom she believed, and therefore, by this faith (Hebrews 11:31), she received them peaceably, though they were enemies of her country.

Lastly, as for that idea of the meritoriousness of the work of Rahab to deserve grace and life eternal, we reject it not only as a vain but as an impious conceit, which never entered into the humble hearts of the saints of old, but has been set on foot in the last corrupt ages of the world by men drunken with self-love and admiration of their own righteousness.

Thus we have these two examples whereby the apostle has proven sufficiently that the faith which is separated from obedience will not justify a man, and therefore that it is a dead faith and not a true living faith according as was promised (James 2:20). Now to close this whole dispute he again repeats that conclusion, adding thereto a new similitude to illustrate it in the last verse of the chapter: "For as the body without the spirit is dead, so faith without works is dead" (James 2:26). That is, as the body without the spirit, i.e., the soul or the breath and other motion, is dead, unable to perform any living action whatsoever, so faith without works is dead, that is, utterly unable to perform these living actions which belong unto it.

What are those actions? There are two. The first is to repose steadfastly upon the promise of life in Christ, which is the proper, immediate living action of faith. The second is to justify a man in the sight of God, which by a special privilege is the consequence of the former. These living actions cannot be performed by that faith which is dead, being destitute of good works. That faith which has no power to bring forth obedience is thereby declared to be a dead faith, devoid of all power to embrace the promise with confidence and reliance, as also to justify.

A man would think this would be plain enough, and does not need to be troubled with any further cavilling. But it is strange what a coil our adversaries make with this similitude, writhing and straining it to such conclusions as the apostle never intended. Whence they gather, first, that as the soul gives life to the body, as the form of the body, so works give life to faith as the form of it. Second, they say that as the body is the same true body without the soul or with it, so faith is one and the same true faith without works or with them. These are nothing but sophistic speculations, far from the purpose of the text. The apostle intends nothing but to show the necessity of linking a living faith and obedience together by the similitude of the like necessity of the union of a living body and the soul. But his purpose is not to show that the manner of their connection is the same, or that just in every point as the soul is to the body or the body to the soul, so works are unto faith and faith unto works. It suffices for his intent that, as in the absence of the soul the body is dead, so in the absence of obedience faith is dead. It does not follow that works, by their presence, do the same things to faith as the soul does to the body by its presence, or that faith in the absence of works remains the same as the body does in the absence of the soul.

If we must be tied to the strict terms of the similitude,

let us examine the comparison a little and we shall see our adversaries all fly off first from it. Let the comparison be made between the body and soul and between faith and works, as the terms are in the text. "As the body without the soul is dead," because the soul gives life, i.e., sense, breathing, and all other motion to the body, "so faith without works is dead," because works give life unto faith (James 2:26). But now this comparison will not run on all fours. For works are not unto faith as the soul is to the body, but as sense and motion are to the body. Since works are external acts, not internal habits, so they are comparable not to the soul, but to the living actions thence issuing. Wherefore it is absurd to say that works give life unto faith, as it is ridiculous to affirm that sense and motion give life to the body, when they are not causes but effects and signs of life. Therefore, when faith without works is dead, it is not spoken in the sense that works give life to faith, as the soul does to the body.

Let then the comparison be between the body and the soul and between faith and charity. As the body without the soul is dead, because the soul is the form of the body and gives life to it, so faith without charity is dead, because charity is the form of faith and gives life to it.

But neither will the comparison hold upon these terms. For, first, our adversaries here mean by "charity" the habit and by "works" the act, which is more than they ought to do, seeing that they would hold us strictly to the very letter of the text. For though we can be content to admit that interpretation if they would admit the apostle's plain meaning and not strain for quirks, yet, considering that they argue so precisely from the words of the comparison, they must not have liberty from us to go with them, but must be content to take the words as they lie in the text and make the best of them. Yet seeing that it is most senseless to make works (that is, external actions) the form of faith (an internal habit), let them take charity instead, an internal habit likewise. Will it be any better now?

Then it is thus: As the soul is the form of the body, so charity is the form of faith; and as the soul gives life and action to the body, so charity gives life unto faith. Will they stand to this?

No. Here again they fly off in both comparisons. Charity is one habit and faith another, different from each other; therefore they deny that there is good reason that charity is either the essential form of faith, as the soul of the living body, or the accidental form, as whiteness of paper. They say it is only an external form.

But this now is not to keep close to the apostle's comparison, but to run from it at their pleasure when they fall upon an absurdity in pressing it so strictly. The soul is not external, but an internal essential form, and therefore charity must be so, if all will match up. Again, does charity give life or living actions unto faith as the soul does unto the body? Neither dare they hold close to this comparison. For the proper work or action of faith is to assent unto the truth of divine revelations because of God's authority, as they themselves teach. Whence now comes this assent? From the habit of faith, or of charity? They grant that it comes immediately from the habit of faith, which produces this action, even when it is severed from charity. Then it is plain that it is not charity which gives life to faith, when faith can perform the proper action that belongs to it, without help.

How then does charity give life unto faith? For this they have a silly conceit. Charity gives life, that is, merit, unto faith. The belief or assent unto divine truth is meritorious if it is with charity. If without charity, then it is not meritorious.

This is a fine toy, wherein again they run from the comparison of the apostle. For the soul gives living actions to the body, not only the qualification of the action; and so charity is not like the soul, because it gives only the qualification of merit unto the action of faith and not the action itself. Besides being a most vain interpretation, it is without any ground from Scripture to say that a living faith is a meritorious faith, when even in common sense the life of any habit consists only in a power to produce those actions that naturally and immediately depend upon that habit.

And what reason is there in the world why the habit of charity should make the actions of faith meritorious, or why charity should make faith meritorious, rather than faith make charity meritorious, since in this life there is no such preeminence of charity above faith? Wherefore we despise these speculative sophisms which, with much fair glossing, our adversaries draw from the text; when all comes to the trial, they themselves will not stand to the strict application of the similitude because it breeds absurdities which even they abhor.

Now if they take liberty to qualify and interpret, they must give us leave to do so too; or, if they will not, we shall take it. To conclude all, this other argument is as weak as the former, namely that a dead body is a true body, and therefore a dead faith is a true faith. This argument forces the similitude and so is unnatural. In material things which have a different being from different causes, it may hold. But it is not so in virtues and graces. Truth and life are both essential to such qualities. True charity is a living charity, i.e., active, as the apostle himself proves in verses

15–16. True valor, like every other virtuous quality, if it is true, is living and stirring in action; if it is otherwise, it is counterfeit, some other thing that has only a shadow of it.

All these tricks are put upon the apostle to pervert his plain meaning, that as it is necessary to the existence of a living body that it be coupled with the soul, so it is necessary to the existence of a living true Christian faith that it bring forth works of obedience.

SECTION VII

Chapter 17

None can be justified by their own satisfaction for the transgression of the law; also, a brief summary of popish doctrine concerning human satisfaction for sin

Thus we have a resolution of the dispute of St. James, together with such cavils as our adversaries make upon the several passages thereof. By the whole order whereof it appears sufficiently that St. James, when disputing against faith, means thereby that false and bastard faith which hypocrites pleased themselves with instead of a true faith, and that, when arguing for works, he means nothing but a working faith. And it appears also that the drift of the apostle in this passage is not to dispute directly of man's justification, but only to bring that in as an argument to prove his conclusion that faith without works is dead because it will not justify. In sum, it is evident that Paul and James do not disagree between themselves, nor does either of them agree with our adversaries in teaching justification by the works of the moral law. Of the impossibility of man's justification by this means, we will speak hitherto.

The next proposition is that none can be justified by their own satisfaction for the transgression of the law. For this is the only way left for an offender to obtain justification and absolution, to allege that he has satisfied for the offense he committed by doing or suffering as much as the party offended could in justice exact of him. This satisfaction being made, he is no longer a debtor unto him, but deserves his absolution and his favor, as if he had not offended at all.

Now, then, the question is whether a sinner may, by anything done or endured by himself, satisfy the justice of God, and so obtain absolution at the bar of God's judgment. We defend the negative, that it is impossible for a sinner by any action or suffering of his own to do so much as shall be equivalent unto the wrong which he has done unto the glorious justice of God, that therewith he may rest satisfied and require no further penalty.

This point is so evident unto the conscience of everyone who knows himself to be either a creature or a man or a sinner that it needs no confirmation. If we are considered as creatures, there is nothing that a finite strength in a finite time can perform which can hold proportion with an offense against an infinite goodness and justice, and with the eternal punishment thereby deserved. Consider us as men, and we are bound to fulfill the law of God in all perfection; nor is there anything so true, so honest, so just, so pure, so worthy of love and good report but the law in one way or another obliges us unto the thought and practice of it.

So that, besides our due debt of obedience, we have nothing to spare over and above whereby to satisfy God for those trespasses that we have committed upon His honor and justice.

Lastly, consider us as sinners, and we are tied in a double obligation—first, of punishment to be suffered for sin committed; second, of obedience to be perpetually performed. Both these debts of punishment and obedience are equally exacted of sinful men, and therefore it is as absurd in divinity to say the obedience of the law or good works will satisfy for the transgression of the law as it is in civil dealing to account the payment of one bond as the discharge also of another. Wherefore everyone who is not blind and proud of heart will here be soon persuaded to relinquish all claims to heaven by his own satisfaction, running unto Him only who alone, without the help of man or angels, has trodden the winepress of the fierceness of God's wrath, bearing our sins in His body on the tree, suffering the utmost, whatsoever was due for the punishment of them.

Our adversaries in this business are in a quandry, mistrusting their own satisfactions, yet not daring wholly to trust Christ's. They will give Him leave to have His part, but by His leave they will have a share too in satisfying for sins. For they are a generation of men who are resolved to be as little beholden to God as possible for grace or for glory. And if there is any article of religion wherein Scripture and reason would give the honor of all unto God, they look at it with an evil eye and cast about which way to thrust themselves in as partners. It is strange to see to what pass pride and covetousness have brought the doctrine of satisfaction as it is now taught and practiced in the Romish Church. With your patience I shall take a short survey of it that you may see which of the two of us rests our consciences upon the surer and more steadfast anchor: we who trust only in Christ's satisfactions, or they who join their own together with His.

The sum of their doctrine, as it is delivered unto us by the Council of Trent (Section 6, chapters 14–16; Section 14, chapters 8–9), with the Romish Catechism (Part 2,

None Can Be Justified by Their Own Satisfaction

chapter 5, questions 52 and following), and explained at large by Bellarmine in his two books *On Purgatory,* in his fourth book *On Penance,* and his book *On Indulgences,* is this:

Sins are of two sorts: first, sins committed before baptism, such as original sin in all who are baptized infants, and actual sins in those who are baptized at the age of discretion; second, sin committed after baptism, when, after the grace of the Holy Ghost has been received in baptism, men fall into sin, polluting the temple of God and grieving His Spirit.

As for the former sort of sins, they are agreed that men are freed from both the fault and punishment of them by the merits and satisfaction of Christ only, without any satisfaction on our part.

But now, for sins after baptism, in obtaining remission of them, Christ and we share responsibility. This partnership is declared unto us in this manner. In these sins (we must know) there are three important components:

1. The fault in the offense against God's majesty and violation of our friendship with Him. Here they grant also that man cannot satisfy for the fault, doing anything that may appease God's displeasure and procure His love. Christ alone has done this for us, for whose satisfaction God of His mercy freely returns into favor and friendship with us. But this must be understood in a Catholic sense, that is, for fault of mortal sins. As for venial sins, God is but slightly angry with them, and so we may satisfy Him for fault thereof both in this life and in purgatory.

2. The stain or corruption of sin, called "the relics of sin abiding in the soul." To purge this there is great force in such satisfactions as are made by prayers, fasting, almsdeeds, and other laborious works, although the heretics

say otherwise. The abolishing of inherent corruption is, by the gift of grace, freely bestowed on us by degrees in the use of all godly means.

3. The punishment of sin, which, after the fault is pardoned, remains yet to be suffered. For although it is true that God in some cases pardons both fault and punishment wholly, as in cases of martyrdom, which sweeps all clean and makes all reckonings even, and although God might have, if it had so pleased Him, always for Christ's sake pardoned the whole debt, yet Holy Mother Church has determined that He does usually do so. But after in mercy He has forgiven the fault, yet there is a later reckoning, and we must come to the bar of God for that punishment, by which His justice is to receive satisfaction. But (you must know) the punishment of sins is twofold.

First, punishment is eternal. The destruction of soul and body in hellfire is to endure forever. Here Christ's satisfaction comes in again, by whose merits alone, they grant, we are delivered from the eternity of the punishment of sin. It must be noted that Christ's satisfaction has not eased us of the substance of the punishment itself, but only in the continuance of it.

Second, punishment is temporal, to endure only for a time, whereof there are also two degrees.

1. One is in this life, as for example all calamities and afflictions upon the body, soul, name, goods, etc., together with death, the last and greatest of evils. All these are inflicted upon man as punishment of sin.

Of these some come upon us inevitably, as death upon all men, or as death in the wilderness on the children of Israel, with the like punishments, certainly and irrevocably pronounced. Now here there is no remedy but patience, and that is an excellent remedy too. For (as the ghostly fathers of Trent inform us) if they are borne willingly with patience, they are satisfaction for our sins, but if unwillingly they are God's just revenge upon us.

Others come evitably—that is, they can be avoided. And here such a course may be taken that we need not suffer the punishment itself, but we may buy it out and make satisfaction for it unto God by other means, which means are principally four.

(1) By the vehemence of contrition or inward sorrow, which may be so intense as to satisfy for all punishments both in this life and also in purgatory.

(2) By other outward laborious works, whereby we may buy out the obligation to temporal punishments. Such works are these:

Prayer with confession, thanksgiving, etc. For if we believe the Catholic doctors, it is a very good satisfaction to a creditor if the debtor prays unto him for the forgiveness of his debt, according to that text, "Call upon Me in the day of trouble, and I will deliver thee" (Psalm 50:15). Therefore, prayer is a satisfaction for the punishment of sin.

Fasting, under which is comprehended the sprinkling of ashes, wearing of hair cloth, whippings, going barefoot, and such other penal works. These also satisfy for sins, as it is written, "David fasted, lay upon the ground and wept all night" (2 Samuel 12:16). Therefore he satisfied for his sins of murder and adultery. And again, Paul says, "I beat down my body" (1 Corinthians 9:27). That is, "I whip and cudgel myself to satisfy for my sins." And again, "The publican smote upon his breast" (Luke 18:13); therefore corporal chastisement is a good satisfaction for sins.

Alms-deeds, comprehending all kinds of works of mercy. These also buy out the punishments of sin, according to the text, "Break off thy sin by righteousness, and thine iniquity by showing mercy towards the poor" (Daniel 4:27). That is, by alms-deeds satisfy for the temporal punishments of your sins. And again, "Give alms of that which you have, and behold, all things shall be clean unto you" (Luke 11:41). That is to say (in the language of Babel), the temporal punishment of sin shall be taken away.

Now all such works as these are either voluntary or enjoined by the priest.

Voluntary works are those undertaken of our own accord, such as voluntary pilgrimages, scourgings, fasts, wearing of sackcloth, weeping, and prayers of such a number and measure, with the like rough punishments which we take upon ourselves to pacify God. All these, being done with an intent to satisfy for the punishment of our sins, must be accepted by God as good payment, because in so doing we do more than He has required of our hands. Now it is very pleasing to God to do what He bids us not, or to do what He bids us toward another end of our own devising. He therefore who voluntarily undertakes such needless pains gives God high satisfaction, according to the text: "If we would judge ourselves, we should not be judged" (1 Corinthians 11:31).

There are also works enjoined by the priest, who, by virtue of the keys committed unto him, might judicially absolve the penitent from the whole debt, were it not thought fit upon special considerations to keep back a part. Wherefore, when he has absolved him from the fault and eternal punishment, he binds him unto satisfaction for the temporal punishment; and therefore he enjoins him what he shall do to buy it out. Let him go visit the shrine of such and such a saint, say so many *Aves* and *Paternosters* before such an image, whip himself so many

None Can Be Justified by Their Own Satisfaction

times, fast so many days, give so much alms, or pay such like penalties.

And when he, in humble obedience, has done these things commanded by the priest, then it is certain that his sins are satisfied for. For it is to be noted that in enjoining this "canonical satisfaction," as it is called, the priest and God Almighty are exactly of the same mind.

Look how much the priest enjoins for satisfaction; God must be content to take the same, or else the penitent's conscience will not be quiet because he would wonder if God expected more to be done for satisfaction than the party has done by the priest's injunction. But it is to be supposed that, like the pope, so every priest in his chair of confession has an infallible spirit whereby he is able to exactly calculate the just proportion between the sin and the punishment, as well as the price of the punishment, so that he may enjoin just so much penance as will buy it out—neither more, lest the penitent be wronged, nor less, lest God be not satisfied. All this is trimly founded upon that text which says, "Whatsoever ye bind on earth shall be bound in heaven; whatsoever ye loose on earth shall be loosed in heaven" (Matthew 16:19; 18:18). That is, priests may forgive the fault and retain the punishment, and what satisfaction they enjoin on earth to expiate the punishment God will accept in heaven. Or else they are deceived. This is the second means to satisfy for temporal punishments.

(3) By pardons and indulgences, wherein the superabundant merits of Christ and His saints are, out of the treasury of the Church, granted by special grace of the Bishop of Rome unto such as are liable to suffer the temporal punishment of their sins. So that they, having gotten by his grant a sufficient portion of satisfactory works out of

the common stock, are freed thereby from satisfying God's justice by their own works, which is a rare privilege, no doubt.

(4) By another living man's satisfaction for them, for not only the superabundant works of Christ and saints departed, but the good works of just men alive will satisfy for another, being done with that intent. So great is God's clemency towards good Catholics that though one man cannot confess nor be contrite for another, yet he may satisfy the justice of God for his sins. Both of these means are grounded upon pregnant places of Scripture: "Bear ye one another's burden" (Galatians 6:2), that is, satisfy for one another. "I will most gladly bestow and be bestowed for your sake" (2 Corinthians 12:15), that is, to satisfy for your sins. "I suffered all things for the elect's sake, and fulfill the rest of the afflictions of Christ in my flesh, for His body's sake, which is the Church" (2 Timothy 2:10; Colossians 1:24)); that is, Paul's sufferings with Christ's sufferings make up a treasury for the Church, so that such as want of their own may make use of Christ's satisfaction and Paul's too. "We being many are one another's members" (Romans 12:5); therefore we may impart satisfactory works one to another, as one member brings heat to another. To conclude, our creed says, "I believe in the communion of saints"; therefore there is a communion of satisfactions. And so the point is very fitly proved, whereby it appears that the children of the Romish Church are reasonably well provided with means to recompense God's justice, and to redeem the temporal punishment for their sins in this life.

2. The other degree of the temporal punishment is in the life to come, namely, in purgatory, whereinto they all drop—those who die in venial sins, the fault whereof was

not forgiven in this life, or in mortal sins, the fault whereof was forgiven in this life, but for which full satisfaction was not made for the punishment before death. Such must fry a while in purgatory, a longer or shorter time according as their sins are more or less heinous, or as men's hearts on earth are more or less pitiful towards them. But, however, there they must be till the temporal punishment of their sins is fully suffered, or bought out by something else that may satisfy God's justice.

This punishment of sin inflicted in purgatory is twofold:

Pena damni, of loss, for example, of the beautiful visions of God and joys of heaven.

Pena sensus, a sense of pain, the bitter pains of God's wrath sensibly tormenting the powers of the soul, inflicted upon them either immediately by God Himself or by the ministry of the devils as His instruments.

For it is a doubt not yet resolved among the patrons of purgatory whether the devils are represented there also as well as in hell. But whether their tormentors are devils or not, this much is agreed upon, that the torment and punishment which the souls suffer in purgatory is as to its substance the very same as the torments of hell, differing only from it in continuance—those of purgatory are temporal; those of hell are eternal. Well, now, such as have not behaved well in this life, to make all even by full satisfaction, must be arrested in halfway to heaven and cast into this prison. Out of this place there are two means by which a person can be delivered.

The first way is by suffering all this temporal punishment for so many years and days as it is to continue. How many that is, you must inquire of St. Michael; the Church knows not. But yet she is sure that many souls shall continue in purgatory till the day of judgment; so there shall be the same period of the world and of their torments. These have a hard time of it; it is easier perhaps with others. But be it as it will be, such as these pay the utmost farthing where they endure in the flames of purgatory until the time of their whole punishment runs out. Then God is satisfied and they are delivered.

The second way is by buying out this punishment by some other satisfactory price. For although God could have so ordered that every soul, being once in purgatory, should suffer all the temporal punishments due, yet He is content to be entreated to commute penance and take some other valuable consideration by way of satisfaction for this punishment.

But this satisfactory payment cannot be made by the souls themselves; it must be made by some on earth for them, which is done either by laborious works of any one just and godly Catholic (whether he is a friend of the deceased or otherwise touched with a charitable pity toward a poor soul, and thus, by his store of devout prayers, alms, masses, pilgrimages, founding of convents and hospitals, etc., may procure a delivery from jail for that soul for whom he intends those good works), or by the pope, who is purse-bearer to the Church and has the treasury thereof under lock and key. Now though he cannot directly absolve the souls in purgatory from their punishment, as he can of men living on the earth, yet he may help them in another way by bestowing on them so much of the superfluous sufferings of Christ and of the saints that thereby God's justice may be satisfied for the whole punishment, which otherwise they should have endured.

Yea, such is the power of his indulgences to infuse virtue into such and such altars, shrines, prayers, etc., that

None Can Be Justified by Their Own Satisfaction

whosoever shall frequent such places or use such prayer, all complements duly observed, may at his pleasure free one, two, three, or more souls out of purgatory. Nay, did not covetousness cool the heat of his apostolic charity, he might so bountifully pour out the treasures of the Church upon these prisoners in purgatory that they should all have enough to weigh down the scales and deserve a passport for heaven. Such efficacy there is in that spiritual pick-lock which the pope has in his keeping. All this is very properly proved by the former places of Scripture, and others also, were it needful now to allege them. But thus we see the Catholics are in every way furnished for satisfactions, so that what Christ has not done for them they can do for themselves, either to suffer and overcome the temporal punishments of their sins, or else, which is the easier course, to buy out that punishment at a valuable price of other satisfactory works, wherewith God's justice shall be abundantly content.

Now whereas those whom they term heretics cry out aloud that such satisfactions of God's justice are indeed no satisfaction at all, because they are in no way equal to the offense committed, and so are no full recompense of wrong offered unto God—to repel this objection, they give us this distinction that they say is very necessary to be observed: satisfaction is of two types.

First, there is a satisfaction of justice consisting in a perfect equality between the offense and the wrong, and the recompense made when so much is done or suffered as the offended party can in justice exact. Now they grant that man cannot satisfy God in this way in the rigor of justice. Only Christ has satisfied so; for unto such a satisfaction it is required that it be done, first, by that which is our own, second, by that which is not already in debt, and, third, by that which is of equal worth and value.

Now in none of these ways can our satisfaction pass in strict justice, because whatsoever we have is God's free gift. Whatsoever we can do is our due obedience; and when we have done all, yet we cannot, by any finite act, do such honor to God as shall be equal to that injury we have offered to His infinite majesty. Even the light of nature teaches, as Bellarmine grants, that man cannot give back equally to God, or give Him *quid pro quo*.

Second, there is a satisfaction of favorable acceptance, wherein there is a kind of imperfect proportion between the offense and the recompense, when so much is done or suffered as God is content in gentleness to take for good satisfaction. Thus, then, a man may satisfy God's justice because God gives him grace to do the amount that He will accept for satisfaction. This grace is threefold:

There is, first, the grace of justification, whereby the Holy Ghost dwells in us and we are made members of Christ, and Christ becomes our Head. By means of this union with Christ, and by the indwelling of the Spirit, it comes to pass that our works have a singular virtue. For Christ communicates unto us His satisfaction, and, by merit of them, makes our works meritorious and satisfactory unto God. So that, whereas whatever things we could have done were of no worth at all in the sight of God, now Christ has earned such a grace for us that the spotted rags of our righteousness and our good works, being dyed in the blood of Christ, receive such a color that they will pass for reasonably good cloth. In a word, our money is now good silver which before was but brass. Again, because the Holy Ghost dwells in the just, therefore (as Bellarmine profoundly argues) their works proceeding from the Holy Ghost have a kind of infiniteness in them, and thereby a

None Can Be Justified by Their Own Satisfaction

kind of equality with the injury which by sinning we offered unto God. It is as much as one might say that a fly or a spider is a kind of infinite creature because it is of God's making and God is infinite. This is the first grace of justification.

There is, second, the grace of evangelical counsels. For although God might rightly claim all our works as due unto Him, yet He does not command all, but only persuades and exhorts in some cases. By this bounty of God, it comes to pass that we have certain works that are of our own, and which we owe Him not, and by these alone we can make satisfaction. Yea, such is the bounty of God that He suffers us to merit by those things which He has given us as His free gift, and is willingly content that what we receive at His hand we give back again to Him as a satisfactory payment to His justice. This is very strange, I tell you.

There is, lastly, one more grace that God gives us; namely, when He pardons the fault He removes the eternity of the punishment and makes it temporal so that it may be more easily satisfied for.

All these particulars and privileges are sure and certain, the Catholic doctors say, because they have firmly proved them out of their own heads without the help of the Scriptures. So, then, they agree that our works are not satisfactory in the rigor of justice, but claim that they are satisfactory to win favorable acceptance by the grace given to do them, and God's clemency in accepting them being done.

Chapter 18

All sin is remitted unto us wholly in the fault and punishment by the satisfaction of Jesus Christ alone

Thus I have at some length set forth unto you the popish doctrine of human satisfaction for sin, wherein it is plain to all who can see anything that their aim has been to lay a plot to delude men's souls and their purses. It would require a large discourse to prosecute their arguments whereby they cover their fraud. But they are not worth spending time on; we must hasten to other matters. The sum of them all comes to this:

1. Those afflictions and temporal chastisements which God has laid upon His children (for the trial of their faith and patience, for their humiliation for sins past by hearty repentance, for their admonition for the time to come, for the examples of others, and so on) must be, in these men's imaginations, true satisfactions to God's justice to expiate their past sins.

2. Such good works as the godly have performed declare their piety, to testify to their thankfulness unto God, to express their sorrow of heart, to bring themselves to a greater measure of true humiliation by much prayer and fasting, to obtain victory over some corruption and temptation, to get some grace which they wanted, to prepare themselves for judgment—all this now must be conceived presently to be meritorious and satisfactory to God's justice for sin.

3. Such penance as in the primitive church was enjoined unto those who, after their conversion and baptism, relapsed again into heathenism, or who for other such scandalous offenses were excommunicated—I say, such penance enjoined to these persons for testifying to their hearty sorrow for their offense, and for satisfaction to the congregation before they might be again admitted into it, must now be turned into a direct and proper satisfaction for the sin itself.

4. Such indulgence or favor as was then sometimes granted toward such relapsed and excommunicated persons (in remitting unto them some part of their enjoined penance upon evident tokens of their unfeigned repentance) is now turned by these men quite to another use, namely to freeing men from further satisfaction to God's justice by applying unto them certain fanatical supererogations treasured up in the pope's cabinet.

These are the many issues and errors of their disputes, wherein I will proceed no further, but only lay down one general conclusion opposite to their doctrine, and so end this point with a few reasons to confirm this truth and confute their error.

The position is this: **All sin whatsoever, original or actual, is remitted unto us wholly with regard to its fault and punishment, temporal as well as eternal, only by the satisfaction of Jesus Christ, and not by any satisfaction made by us unto the justice of God.** To confirm this sacred truth, delivered unto us in the Word and generally embraced by the Reformed churches (and even by our adversaries themselves when the agonies of conscience, the apprehension of death, and God's judgment do clear up their eyes a little to behold the vanity of their poor satisfaction), we observe these reasons:

REASON 1. The first reason is that the innumerable testimonies of Scripture ascribe the remission of sin only to the mercy of God in Christ crucified. Christ has borne our sins (1 Peter 2:24); His blood has purged us of all sin (Hebrews 1:3); His death redeemed us from all iniquity (Titus 2:24)); His stripes healed us (Isaiah 53:5; 1 Peter 1:24); He has paid the price of our ransom (1 Timothy 2:6); God for His sake has forgiven us our trespasses and blotted out our sins (Colossians 2:13–14); God has cast our sins behind His back (Isaiah 38:17); and God has forgotten our sins (Jeremiah 31:34). With the store of such sayings, the doing away of all sins is ascribed to the grace of God through the satisfaction of Christ, without limiting it to any sin or mentioning any satisfactory works of ours.

Now what do our adversaries say to this? By a shift they turn aside all the Scripture tending to this purpose. Thus Christ has satisfied for the fault of our sins and reconciled us unto God, and has also satisfied for the eternity of the punishment. But He has not satisfied for the temporal punishment; we must endure torments, though but for a while. This is a mere cavil without any apparent ground from such texts of Scripture, or necessary deduction from others. We deny it therefore, as they affirm it.

And, that it may appear to be but a forged device, let us invert the distinction and we shall hold it with as good probability the other way. Christ satisfied for the fault, but not for the punishment, they say. Let us suppose the reverse and say that Christ satisfied for the punishment, but not for the fault. We, by our own satisfaction, must procure God's favor. Now let them object what they can against this. If we wish to cavil as they do, we can deflect their objections with as fair probability as they do our arguments on the other part. Let them name all the places

All Sin Is Remitted Due to Christ's Satisfaction

that say Christ has reconciled us unto God, His Father (Colossians 3:20). This is easily put off. Christ has reconciled us; that is, Christ deserved such grace for us that we by our works may reconcile ourselves. (This is just as when they say Christ has satisfied, that is, procured grace for us that we by our works might satisfy.) Let them object that our works can be of no worth to appease God's anger; we will say it is true that of themselves they are not, but Christ has merited that they should be of sufficient worth. (This is just as they say unto us, when we object that our works are not of value to satisfy God's justice, that they say of themselves they are not but Christ has deserved for them to make them satisfactory.) Thus if every idle distinction not fortified by necessary deduction from Scripture might pass for a good answer, the certainty of divine doctrine would soon be shaken to pieces, and no position would be too absurd to be defended with much facility.

REASON 2. That assertion of theirs, namely that the fault is forgiven and the punishment required, is most false and absurd, even in common sense. To pardon a fault and be friends, and yet require full satisfaction; to forgive the debt, yet to exact the payment—are not these empty kindnesses? Bellarmine tells us there are some offenses of so grievous a nature that satisfaction cannot be made except over a long period of time. Now in this case the party wronged may pardon the other, and be reconciled to him, yet the offender remains bound to make entire satisfaction for the wrong. But now the Jesuit does not name any such case, neither indeed can he. For suppose a subject has offended his prince and the fault deserved seven years of solitary imprisonment for satisfaction. If the prince should say unto him, "I pardon your offense; you have my love, but yet you shall stay in prison till the last day," would it not be a mockery? Would any man thank him for such a kindness? The Jesuits, the incendiaries of Christendom, would not thank Christian princes for such a courtesy, if they should pardon them their fault and then hang them. There is an equal absurdity in this, when they say that after the fault is pardoned, yet in this life and in purgatory the temporal punishment must be suffered. Why must it by suffered? For satisfaction, they say. Of what? Of God's justice. For what now? Is it for the fault and offense committed? No, that is pardoned. For what then? For just nothing.

Again this assertion is contrary to good reason. For God's friendship and His justice may not be divided in this way, as if He were reconciled and well pleased with that creature which has violated His justice and not made satisfaction for it. God's friendship with man follows satisfaction to His justice, even as His enmity with man is a consequence of the breach of His justice. His righteous will is transgressed; therefore He is offended. His righteous will must be satisfied before He is pleased. So that it is a vain speculation to think that Christ has appeased God's anger but not satisfied His justice, forasmuch as His favor is purchased only by satisfaction of His justice offended.

REASON 3. This doctrine of human satisfactions obscures the dignity and overthrows the force of Christ's satisfaction. If we have a share, then He does not have all the glory. No, He has scarcely any at all. For, we ask, what has Christ satisfied? They say that He has procured God's love for us. But that cannot be unless He has satisfied His justice. Has He done this or not? Yes, He has satisfied for the eternity of the punishment. Yes, but how do they know that? What if we, upon their ground, say that He has not

All Sin Is Remitted Due to Christ's Satisfaction

satisfied for the eternity of it, but only merited that our sufferings and satisfactions should be equivalent to the eternity of the punishment?—especially considering that our works, according to Bellarmine, have a certain kind of infinite value in them.

Again, eternity is but an incidental characteristic of punishment of sin; the essentials of it are the loss of joy and the sense of pain. If therefore Christ has satisfied only for that, He has done but the least part. Nevertheless, our adversaries will need to persuade us that human satisfaction does not so much eclipse as illustrate the glory of Christ's satisfactions, inasmuch as thereby He has not only rendered satisfaction Himself, but also made us able to satisfy. A great matter, doubtless. But where do the Scriptures say any such matter, that Christ has merited so that we might merit and satisfy? Moreover, by this trick, while Christ makes us able to merit and satisfy, His own satisfaction is plainly excluded. For come to the point and ask, "Who satisfies God's justice for sin, Christ or us?"

Here Bellarmine stumbles like a blind horse, and of three answers takes the very worst. He explains that some say it is Christ, and He alone satisfies properly, but we improperly, our works being only a condition without which Christ's satisfaction is not applied to us. But such smells of the fagot, for it is a perilous heresy to say, "Christ alone satisfies for sins." Others say that both Christ and we ourselves satisfy, and that there are two satisfactions for the same offense. But this metal does not clink well either.

Wherefore others are of the opinion, and Bellarmine likes it, that we alone satisfy Christ. He says this third method seems most probable—a method which basically entails one actual satisfaction, and that satisfaction would be ours. Yea, this is as it should be: thrust out Christ and let us alone satisfy while He stands by and holds the candle. Yet the Jesuit will not do Jesus so much wrong, for mark, to mend the matter he adds, "No, Christ is not shut out, nor His satisfaction. For through His satisfaction we have grace, whence we make satisfaction. And by this means Christ's satisfaction is said to be applied to us—not because His satisfaction itself immediately lifts due temporal punishment from us, but because it mediately lifts it, in so far as we have grace, without which our satisfaction would avail us nothing."

These words they may understand, but I cannot. The Jesuit walks in the dark, seeking to hide this shameful injury to the merits of Christ, but it will not be. It is too apparent that Christ is to them of no account. Only for a fashion they make use of His name, when they have reckoned up a litany of their own merits, and saints' merits, and such other trash, then to conclude all with "Through Jesus Christ our Lord." That is the burden of the song, and the oil that seasons all the salad, Marnix merrily says.

REASON 4. That distinction between satisfaction of strict justice, and satisfaction as favorable acceptance is vain in this business. We grant indeed that our good works done out of faith are pleasing to God and graciously accepted by Him; but can it appear that God accepts them as satisfaction of His justice? No Scripture intimates any such thing, that God's favor thus dispenses with His justice and makes that satisfaction acceptable which is, in itself, no full satisfaction of His justice. Shall we think that God in this case is put upon those terms of necessity and negotiation which fall out in human satisfaction between man and man? It may so fall out that a creditor to whom a thousand crowns are owing may be content if the debtor will yield up his whole estate, though not worth fifty, be-

All Sin Is Remitted Due to Christ's Satisfaction

cause no more can be had. So, in case of offense, a word or two of confession of the wrong may be accepted for satisfaction. But God lacks no means to receive full satisfaction of us, either upon our own persons or upon Christ for us. And therefore it is without ground to imagine such a weakness and partiality of His justice as to be satisfied with a few poor, compensatory formalities. For satisfaction of God's justice, we acknowledge nothing but such as is in justice sufficient. Such are Christ's satisfactions. But, as for us, we have nothing to do with satisfaction but with free pardon.

REASON 5. This doctrine of human satisfaction taught in the Church of Rome is altogether full of uncertainty, and therefore brings no rest and peace unto men's consciences at all. "God pardons the fault, but requires the punishment," they say. But when is this? Is it always? No, sometimes He pardons both. But can they tell certainly when He does and when He does not? "At martyrdom He pardons all." How do they know that? Or how do they know that He does not do the same at other times too? "Contrition," they say, "if it is vehement, satisfies for all." But can they tell us the just measure of that contrition which is satisfactory? It may be that the party is contrite enough, yet the priest enjoins penance when it is needless. It may be that he is not contrite enough, yet no penance is enjoined. Where is the certainty, and what is to be done in such a case? "Christ," they say, "has satisfied for the eternity of hell punishment." Well enough. But can they tell how many years or days are left unsatisfied for, that all things may be fitted according to the race of time? "Laborious works of prayer, fasting, and alms-deeds satisfy for temporal punishments in this life," they say. Suppose it to be so. Are they sure they can also satisfy the pains of purgatory? The priest enjoins satisfactory penance. But is he sure that he enjoins just so much as will do the feat? Is he certain that God will take that for payment which he decrees to be paid? What if there are not enough *Ave Marias,* and so forth?

Again, suppose there were evangelical counsels, such as to take vows of chastity, poverty, and the like, and that to do these things is pleasing unto God. Are they sure that they should pass for satisfaction in this case? You say that you give alms, vow poverty, do this and that to satisfy God's justice for such or such a sin. What? Is it required that God must do as you desire and take what you offer for payment? Where is the warrant for that? As for those who are in purgatory, when have they satisfied enough? Who brings word when they are delivered? How does the pope know when he has bestowed upon them sufficient supererogative money to pay the fees of the prison? Or does Saint Michael, who holds the scales, send him word when their satisfactions outweigh their sins? Not to belabor the point, but there is in all this doctrine no firm ground whereon a distressed soul may cast anchor; rather, when it has once let slip that main cable on which it might ride out all storms (the satisfaction of Christ), afterwards it is carried adrift upon all hazards of winds and seas.

REASON 6. Their practice betrays their opinion. If they indeed thought that there was any severity in God's justice, any necessity or sufficiency in such satisfactions of theirs, it is not possible that they would prostitute such things in so base a manner as they do. But when an *Ave Maria,* a *Paternoster* before such or such an altar, a wax candle to such a saint, a kiss of such a cold stone, a pilgrimage to Compostella for cockleshells, a lash or two upon the bare back, two or three meals meat forborne, a pardon purchased for a few coins—yea, when the roughness and meanness of Adam's figleaf breeches shall be accounted a worthy matter to satisfy for his sin, as Bellarmine most ridiculously dotes; I say, when such base trifles shall be reckoned to be valuable satisfactions of God's justice, they must pardon us if we guess at their meaning. They may dispute and talk how they will in big words and fair glosses of bridles against sins, and I know not what, but in time, all proves to be but buckets to catch money. But regarding such as serve themselves thus upon God and play with His justice, as the fly with the candle, let them take heed lest in the end they be consumed by it.

To leave, then, these vain inventions, let us give to God the glory that is due His name, and so we shall well provide for the peace of our souls, trusting entirely and only in that name of Jesus Christ besides which there is not in heaven or on earth (in man or angel) any name, merit, power, satisfaction, or anything else whereby we may be saved (Acts 4:12). And so much for the great question of justification by our own righteousness, whereby it appears sufficiently that we shall never be justified in God's sight.